Primary Education — At a Hinge of History?

Colin Richards

FALMER PRESS
Taylor & Francis Group

First published 1999 by Falmer Press
11 New Fetter Lane, London EC4P 4EE

Simultaneously published in the USA and Canada
by Falmer Press
Routledge Inc., 29 West 35th Street, New York, NY 10001

Falmer Press is an imprint of the Taylor & Francis Group

First published in 1999

A catalogue record for this book is available from the British Library

ISBN 0 7507 0986 3 cased
ISBN 0 7507 0985 5 paper

Library of Congress Cataloging-in-Publication Data are available on request

Jacket design by Caroline Archer

Typeset in 10/12pt Times by
Graphicraft Limited, Hong Kong

Printed in Great Britain by Biddles Ltd., Guildford and King's Lynn on paper which has a specified pH value on final paper manufacture of not less than 7.5 and is therefore 'acid free'.

Contents

Contents

Acknowledgments

Some chapters have been published previously, though all have been modified for inclusion in this book. They appeared in print as:

Chapter 1   'At a hinge of history?', *Times Educational Supplement*, 19–4–96
Chapter 2   'Individuality, equality and discovery', *Times Educational Supplement*, 20–1–97
Chapter 3   'Primary education 1974–80', in RICHARDS, C. (ed.) (1982) *New Directions in Primary Education*, London, Falmer Press.
Chapter 4   'Demythologising primary education', *Journal of Curriculum Studies*, **12**, 1, 1980.
Chapter 5   'Primary education in England: An analysis of recent issues and developments', in CLARKSON, M. (ed.) (1988) *Emerging Issues in Primary Education*, London, Falmer Press.
Chapter 7   'Changing elementary/primary curricula: The English experience 1862–2012', in MOYLES, J. and HARGREAVES, L. (eds) (1998) *The Primary Curriculum: Learning from International Perspectives*, London, Routledge.
Chapter 9   'Implementing the National Curriculum at Key Stage 2', *The Curriculum Journal*, **4**, 2, 1993.
Chapter 10   'Curriculum and pedagogy in key stage 2: A survey of policy and practice in small primary schools', *The Curriculum Journal*, **9**, 3, 1998.
Chapter 16   'Subject expertise and its deployment in primary schools', *Education 3–13*, **21**, 1, 1994.
Chapter 17   'A Key Stage 6 core curriculum?', RICHARDS C., HARLING, P. and WEBB, D., Association of Teachers and Lecturers, 1997.
Chapter 18   *'Primary Teaching: High Status? High Standards?'*, in RICHARDS, C., SIMCO, N., and TWISTLETON, S. (eds) (1998) *Primary Teacher Education: High Status? High Standards*, London, Falmer Press.
Chapter 19   'Editorial', *Education 3–13*, **26**, 1, 1998.

Series Editors' Preface

We were delighted when Colin Richards agreed to include this book in the **Primary Directions** series. Colin has considerable experience of primary education from a broad range of perspectives and what is included here is a scholarly and thorough review of the past, present and future of primary education. We believe that this book will become an essential resource for all those who wish to understand the ways in which primary education has changed and the ways in which it might be changing in the future. As he explains, the book is based upon both previously published material and unpublished material originally given as talks or lectures.

As specialist adviser for primary education within Her Majesty's Inspectorate and through active links with the research community, he was able to present a broad, balanced and often positive impression of developments in primary education. However, he began to realize that this was in direct contrast to the 'official' view being expressed by OFSTED. No longer subject to the restraints of OFSTED he has been able to

> ... write what I want both about government policy and about the past, present and the future of primary education, but also of challenge to current government approaches.

As far as the National Curriculum is concerned he suggests that we now have the most demanding primary curriculum anywhere in the world, with more direction, structure and expectation and he argues that revisions to the National Curriculum should be based on a systematic, comprehensive evaluation of 'what is happening at the chalk face'.

Colin offers the book as an opportunity for primary practitioners to make sense of the recent past and

> ... dispel many misconceptions and misunderstandings about primary education as it faces an uncertain future ... Who knows, it might even make a small contribution to the re-education of at least some contemporary critics and proponents of reform.

He accepts that it was and still remains very difficult to give primary education a voice in educational decision making at the national level. This book makes a substantial contribution to that debate and will be of relevance to a wide range of readers — to students in training, to teachers on inservice courses, to lecturers, researchers and to policy-makers, in fact to all those who wish to understand the history and principles upon which primary education has developed.

Colin Conner and Geoff Southworth
February 1999

1 Introduction: Primary Education — At a Hinge of History?

To its cost or benefit, primary education in England is at the centre of political attention. It is seen as crucial to achieving the government's target of driving up educational standards. It is the subject of many initiatives. It is the focus of many criticisms. Yet almost all of its critics and leading proponents of its reform, whether in government, the DfEE, QCA, TTA or OFSTED have little or no background experience in primary education to draw on except presumably as pupils (though not always in the state system) and, in some cases, as parents. They have no first-hand experience of the culture of the primary education they are trying to reform, no empathy with hard-pressed, demoralized primary teachers struggling with an almost impossible job and no understanding of the recent history of primary education with its stresses, pressures, opportunities and enduring myths.

This book provides perspectives on the developing culture and context of primary education since the publication of the Plowden Report in 1967. It analyses and comments on a wide range of issues, many of which are current concerns and remain perennial to the pursuit of primary education. It provides a constructive critique of the development of the National Curriculum and of OFSTED; comments on developments in primary teacher education from the viewpoint of a concerned 'returner' to higher education; and contributes to contemporary debates about primary teaching methodology and the future of primary education from the perspective of someone who, very immodestly, wants his views heard.

The book is based partly on unpublished material, originally written as talks or lectures, and partly on published work; all the chapters have been modified to varying degrees and all, except the historical pieces, have been up-dated. Some of the chapters are contributions to the history of English primary education. Others contribute to current debates and introduce concepts or distinctions to carry that discussion forward. Still others are deliberately speculative and to a degree polemical raising issues about the future of primary education in the medium term. Each chapter in the book is prefaced by a short section in which I put the chapter in the context of developments since 1967: and highlight the significance of the issues it raises.

The main title of the book is taken from this 'Platform' piece published in the Times Educational Supplement in April 1996. I felt it was important to record how primary schools had coped reasonably successfully with the introduction of the National Curriculum and the multitude of other changes consequent on the 1988 Education Reform Act and, very importantly, how they had begun to re-examine many of their long-established assumptions and practices such as topic work, the class-teacher system, grouping practices and other aspects of primary pedagogy. I wanted to paint a picture of a sector 'on the move', self-critical, sceptical towards the 'verities of the past', responsive to change and 'at a hinge in its history'. However, I wanted to draw attention to the deep malaise and demoralization within primary schools. I also wanted to warn against the gathering forces of reaction whose view of primary education was more informed by the realities (and aspirations) of the nineteenth century rather than the late twentieth century and who could turn that 'hinge' backwards to the certainties of a latter-day elementary education rather than forward to confront the challenges and uncertainties of primary education in the early twenty-first century.

I hope that this book will help primary practitioners make sense of the present and recent past and that it will also dispel many misconceptions and misunderstandings about primary education as it faces an uncertain future 'at a hinge in its history'. Who knows, it might even make a small contribution to the re-education of at least some contemporary critics and proponents of reform.

I don't know where the idea of a 'hinge of history' originated but I first used it in 1979 when giving a talk to primary headteachers on developments in the 1980s. I remember making much of the crucial importance of the date on which I gave the talk and then speculating, I believed authoritatively, on a wide range of probable developments. Almost none of my speculations proved correct! My only success was to predict the crucial significance of the date 8 May 1979, the date of the general election which brought the Conservative Party to power. As with hinges which open or shut doors, so that day opened up a wide range of unimagined possibilities and initiatives and shut off others. To use a fashionable cliché it proved 'a defining moment' in the recent history of the education service.

I believe that 17 years on, primary education is again at a 'hinge of history' where possibilities can be opened up or shut down, where policies and practice can move forward or regress. This 'hinge' is not tied to a general election, though one is in the offing. There is a very real paradox. At the very time when primary education is poised to move forward after a decade of far-reaching change, there is a danger of failure of nerve, a possible fateful hesitation, a danger of reversion to the certainties of nineteenth-century education rather than confrontation with the challenges and uncertainties of twenty-first century primary education.

Primary schools generally (though not universally) have achieved much in the decade since 1986. David Bell in the *Times Educational Supplement* (9 February 1996) highlights the successful introduction of the National Curriculum and the implementation of more sophisticated assessment procedures at a time of falling budgets and rising class sizes — achieved without damaging the very positive, motivating atmosphere of so many primary schools. A dispassionate evaluation of evidence from OFSTED and other sources reveals other improvements: the successful introduction of LMS; the development of more effective curriculum coordination and planning; the fostering of closer, more productive links with parents; more systematic approaches to school and staff development. Other improvements could be cited. There is *no* inspection evidence to suggest that these have been achieved at the expense of standards in the so-called but mis-named 'basic skills'; indeed, there is evidence of improvement in children's basic knowledge, understanding and skills related to time, place and the physical/biological world.

Of possibly longer term significance is the questioning of long-established assumptions and practices. In some (though again not all) schools, primary education is being seen, not as an end in itself or merely preparatory to secondary education, but as part of a reasonably consistent, continuous and coherent educational experience offered to pupils from 5 (or earlier) to 16. In some schools, distinctive curricula go well beyond the basic requirements of the National Curriculum. In some, the 'mixed economy' of separate subject work and topic work is being reviewed (though rarely replaced) and separate treatment given to particular aspects of the programmes of study. In some, generalist class teaching is being complemented (but again rarely replaced) by forms of semi-specialist teaching to make better use of the curricular expertise available on the staff. In some, teaching methodology is being 'opened up' to scrutiny; discussion about the relative merits of class, group or individual teaching (a relatively *un*important pedagogic issue) is being extended to a much more valuable examination of the range and quality of teaching techniques to be employed whatever the context. Such questioning of assumptions and practice is necessary if primary education is to move consciously forward, rather than consciously or unconsciously back, into the twenty-first century.

YET, despite some improvement in policy and practice, despite some encouraging signs of a healthy professional scepticism towards the verities of the past, there is a deep malaise within English primary education — a malaise shared by so many heads, teachers, advisers, inspectors and HMI. There is a feeling of disspiritness, a sense of being ill-used by government and by government agencies such as OFSTED; a feeling of being misunderstood and unappreciated by local and national politicians; a sense of being victimized and scape-goated by unsympathetic media and others anxious to denigrate rather than objectively evaluate educational achievement. A decade or more of derision is in danger of corroding the professionalism of so many heads, teachers and inspectors.

This negative tone is captured for me in this year's Annual Report from Her Majesty's Chief Inspector of Schools. The dismal picture it paints of English primary education is not one which I recognize. In my view, it contributes to a deepening, not an alleviation, of the malaise afflicting primary education. It needs to be contested.

The lowering of morale and loss of self-confidence occasioned by this and other examples of negative comment, are particularly regrettable at a time when the rhetoric of the Dearing settlement offers schools the possibility of reclaiming the curriculum and making it to some extent their own through the exercise of professional discretion. That rhetoric needs to be accepted at face value. The discretion it offers needs to be seized and worked upon in school after school despite countervailing pressures such as testing, performance tables and OFSTED's increasing preoccupation with inspecting a core, rather than a broad entitlement, curriculum.

At this hinge of its history, primary education is indeed at a 'defining moment'. Building on the achievements of the last decade and rising to the challenge of discretion, post-Dearing primary schools could develop broad, challenging curricula, perhaps with elements of tailor-made enrichment, which involve a liberal view of what is basic to a child's education and which are taught through a wide variety of techniques in a range of contexts. Or they could lose their nerve and end up providing a curriculum dominated by the 'basic basics' which fails to challenge the multiple intelligences of their pupils and which is delivered by a pedagogy more suited to the nineteenth rather than the twenty-first century.

Will the next decade see the continuing development of a genuine primary education or the re-emergence of neo-elementary schooling?

Part 1

Primary Education:
Towards a Recent History

2   The Plowden Report: Reappraised

The publication of the Plowden Report (Children and their Primary Schools) in 1967 represented a major landmark in the history of English primary education. It represented the high point of political and public interest in primary education in the 50 years following the Second World War. It brought primary education into the limelight. It represented primary education as part of the 'cultural revolution' of the 1960s. It embodied a spirit of optimism, expansion and confidence, far removed from the educational recession and professional depression of the decades that followed. It promised, though was not able to deliver, the end of primary education's 'Cinderella' status within public education. To many, it represented the zenith of the beneficent influence of 'child-centred' education both in terms of official orthodoxy and professional practice. To many others, it represented a pernicious influence which was to weaken educational standards and quality for decades to come. 'Represented' is key to understanding its significance. The Central Advisory Council did not, could not, legislate; it did not make policy; it did not provide resources; it did not administer primary schools. It did, however, represent *and* articulate *the importance of primary education to a degree that no other official reports before or since have done. Throughout the last 30 years it has remained the most quoted text in the canon of primary education. Its influence on professional opinion cannot be denied; its influence on policy and practice is more uncertain and contentious. Only now can its effects be assessed with any degree of objectivity, as this brief appraisal, written in 1997, attempts to do.*

English primary education badly needs appreciating in two senses of the word — a favourable recognition of its achievements and a sensitive understanding and appraisal of its strengths and weaknesses. *Children and their Primary Schools* (the Plowden Report) provided both for primary education in the 1960s. Its celebration of achievement may have been over the top; its appraisal may have been flawed in important respects; and the trends it identified may have failed to materialize, but it stands as a significant landmark in the history of primary education and one which inspired many primary teachers.

It was the Consultative Committee of the Board of Education which, in 1926, first officially recommended the establishment of primary and secondary education as two distinct stages to replace the notion of elementary education. It was the Committee's second report in 1931 (*The Primary School*) which established a rationale for primary education and made recommendations on its curriculum, teaching, organization and staffing based on what was known of children's physical and mental development. It viewed the curriculum *both* in terms of 'activity' and 'experience' but also in terms of 'knowledge to be acquired' and 'facts to be stored'. It acknowledged 'the great and special virtues' of class-teaching but pointed out that there were 'limits to its flexibility and therefore its usefulness' because of the 'varying needs of children or the natural movement of their minds'. If the rest of philosophy can be regarded as footnotes to Plato, then in a very real sense Plowden provided the footnotes to the 1931 report with its developmental emphasis and with its eclectic approach to both curriculum and pedagogy (unacknowledged by many of its critics).

In the intervening period between the publication of the two reports there were many significant events — not least a world war and in education a new act (1944) which formally established primary education as a distinct stage in the English educational system. Post-war, the government's chief concerns for the new sector related to problems of teacher supply, 'roofs over heads' for the fast-burgeoning population of primary-aged pupils and the replacement of 'all-through' schools by primary and secondary provision (a process not completed until after the publication of Plowden). In very many areas junior schools and the junior departments of newly established primary schools were in thrall to the selection examination at 11 plus. Those schools large enough to stream pupils by ability did so. For older primary pupils, in particular, the developments advocated by the 1931 report largely went unrealized; their curriculum remained dominated by the teaching of reading, writing, number and 'intelligence' in preparation for the selection examination.

However, with younger children, a long-established developmental tradition did increase its influence on practice post-war. In many, though not all, infant schools the rigidities of the timetable were dispensed with; work related to centres of interest or topics was introduced; children were given more choice of activities and encouraged to take a measure of responsibility for their own learning; classrooms were reorganized along 'informal' lines; more individual and small group teaching took place; there was an increasing emphasis on methods involving 'discovery', creativity and first-hand experience. Such approaches also began to affect junior-aged pupils in some schools in a number of local education authorities such as Oxfordshire, West Riding, Bristol and Leicestershire. It was developments such as these that Plowden identified as 'a quickening trend' and sought to publicize, celebrate and disseminate for the benefit of all pupils up to the age of 12 (its recommended age of transfer).

There are a number of important general points to be made about the report. First and foremost it was a *serious* attempt 'to consider primary education in all its aspects'. It took over three years to complete; it involved commissioning a great deal of research; it drew on a survey by HMI of *all* English primary schools; it called on oral or written evidence from a very wide range of interested parties; it also involved a small element of comparison with primary education overseas. The Plowden Committee amassed facts, canvassed opinions but was not afraid to make generalizations, judgments and recommendations on the basis of the evidence it had collected. The report provided a rich, detailed, comprehensive appreciation of a developing sector.

Allied to this was the principled approach adopted in the report. It made its underlying values very explicit: equality of opportunity, compensation for handicaps, respect for individuality, and a commitment to the highest educational standards involving 'special stress on individual discovery, on first-hand experience and on opportunities for creative work'. It treated research findings with caution and care; it revealed, rather than hid, the wide spectrum of opinion it solicited but it was not frightened to take its stand in favour of the 'developmental tradition'. It asserted rather too confidently, as it turned out, that 'the gloomy forebodings of the decline of knowledge which would follow progressive methods have been discredited'.

But most amazing of all to the reader who revisits the report after 30 years was its positive, affirmative tone. Not only was the future of English society viewed optimistically, but teachers, schools and, above all, children were valued both for what they had achieved and what they could achieve in the future. The report praised, celebrated, and encouraged. In a number of places its plaudits verged on the hyperbolical and made many readers sceptical of the judgments of the Committee and of the representativeness of the practice it characterized — 'English primary education at its best . . . is very good indeed. Only rarely is it very bad. *The average is good*' (p. 461, my italics).

Partly because of its very positive stance the report was criticized by many practitioners (including me) for being far too utopian. With its composite vignettes of 'good practice' and its inevitably selective use of illustrations to support its aspirations it presented a view of practice far removed from the reality of very many primary teachers toiling with classes of over 40 in urban contexts, coping with the demands (and backlash) of the '11 plus' and very often still imbued with the attitudes, expectations and practices associated with the elementary school tradition. To many, its aspirations, both for them as teachers and for their pupils, appeared utterly remote and unrealistic. To use 1960s' language, it probably put off more teachers than it 'turned on'. In too many cases its advocacy of what it considered excellent practice militated against the generality of practice advancing towards what it would see as good.

One of its most appealing features, its purple prose, proved a mixed blessing since phrases taken out of context could be, and were, seized upon both by its critics and by its uncritical devotees. 'The child is the agent in his own learning', the 'danger sign' of 'much time spent on teaching' and the all-too-confident assertion that 'finding out' has proved to be better for children than 'being told' were seen by some as implying an abdication of the teacher's responsibility to teach. Both the critics and the zealots conveniently forgot other passages: 'from the start there must be teaching as well as learning' or 'we certainly do not deny the value of "learning by description" or the need for practice of skills and consolidation of knowledge'. The devil can quote scripture to suit his purposes; that was also true of both the antagonists and the protagonists of Plowden.

The effects of the report are difficult to summarize. Certainly for some teachers it provided, and still provides, a perennial source of inspiration — a view of what might be possible 'in the best of all possible worlds'. Its support for individuality and creativity led to some outstanding work by individual schools or teachers which demonstrated how untapped by conventional schooling is the potential of so many children. It provided powerful support for the abolition of selection (already gaining ground for other reasons) and it helped remove the widespread practice of streaming by ability and the inequalities and the waste that system of internal organization had wreaked. It transformed the physical layout of many schools and classrooms.

But it had other effects too. The value it placed on individuality led in too many schools to an undue emphasis on individual learning, impossible to implement effectively in all but very small classes, and denying too many children sustained interaction with the teacher and other pupils either as a class or in groups. A minority of teachers did effectively abdicate their responsibilities for teaching. Too often far more attention was paid to the niceties of classroom layout, display and learning environment and not enough attention to the content of the curriculum or the means by which it might be taught. The 'laissez-faire' curriculum of the 1970s and early 1980s owed much to the lack of a firm clear lead from Plowden on curriculum matters. Having said that, there was no significant 'primary school revolution' along Plowden lines; the 'quickening trend' it identified failed to materialize.

The publication of the Plowden Report in 1967 contributed to an exceptional context in which primary schools operated, albeit for a short time only. For a few years, primary education was regarded by government as a particularly important stage in the educational system and primary teachers were made to feel valued and good about themselves and their profession. Those two conditions had not coincided before, they have not coincided since, and they show no signs of coinciding in the future. In retrospect it is clear that Plowden's optimism was misplaced, but far better that misplaced optimism than the misplaced pessimism that I believe so weakens and demoralizes primary education currently.

3   Primary Education 1974–80

In the eyes of some commentators, and in the experience of many primary school teachers, the period 1967–74 following the publication of the Plowden Report was a 'golden age' with primary education receiving much political and public attention and praise, increased resources, promised expansion (especially of nursery education) and a long overdue acknowledgment of its fundamental importance. Paradoxically, in view of her later policies, this trend reached a climax under Margaret Thatcher as Secretary of State when in 1972 her White Paper, the misnamed (as it turned out) Framework for Expansion promised 'to bring about a shift of resources within the education budget in favour of primary schools' at the expense of secondary and higher education.

It was not to be. The most severe economic crisis since before the Second World War put paid to that. Not all those involved in working in, or commentating on, primary education post-Plowden would have accepted the image of the 'golden age', but virtually all would agree that the succeeding years were the beginning of the age of disillusionment — with the social democratic consensus, with the state of the economy, with the condition of the public services, with the contribution of the education system, with the quality of primary education and with the work of primary school teachers. It is fashionable to mark the beginning of this period 'of discontent' with education by the Prime Minister's Ruskin College speech of 1976, but as far as primary education is concerned its roots can be traced back earlier — to 1974. The themes of the next six years — demographic, economic and educational contraction, increasing governmental involvement, accountability and monitoring of the system — developed from that year onwards and gradually established their grip on political and professional consciousness and on educational decision-making. This chapter, written in 1981, provides a synoptic view of the latter half of the 1970s.

Starting Point

Normally within the state system a child's primary education lasts for a minimum of six years. Except for those now in middle schools, children who entered reception classes as 5-year-olds in 1974 emerged as primary leavers in 1980. During that six-year period the children themselves are unlikely to have been conscious of many changes (except in their own capabilities), though in fact the pressure on their playground and hall space may have eased, the number of new teachers per year may have fallen and the number of 'dinner ladies' and 'helpers' in their school may have been reduced. Class teachers during that same period are more likely to have noticed a marked increase, followed by a decline, in the purchasing power of their salaries, a reduction in available resources and support services, an increase in union activity, a reduction in promotion prospects and a general increase in dissatisfaction and unease. Heads are very likely to have become aware of changes in their school's economic and 'political' circumstances: in particular, a marked reduction in resources which could be purchased through capitation allowances and an increase in parental concern about the achievements of pupils. All such changes have not affected every school and every teacher, but many have had an effect. They are illustrative of more general tendencies which have made the period 1974–80 very different from the corresponding period in the previous decade.

Providing an overview of such general developments is not easy when there are some 20,000 English primary schools and some 200,000 teachers and especially when 'there is a sense in which there is not a system in Britain, but rather a legal framework within which many independent bodies operate' (Peston, 1979, p. 11). However, without some such overview it is difficult to relate one development to another or to relate particular instances to more general tendencies. What follows is a tentative attempt to provide a backcloth against which some new directions in English primary education can be identified. With its mixture of facts and impressions the account tries to indicate ideas in currency and issues in context; it does not claim to be based on what was actually happening in *all* 200,000 classrooms.

The choice of 1974 as the starting point for this analysis is a deliberate one. In the decade prior to 1974, primary education began to shed something of its 'Cinderella' status. Between 1960 and 1974, capital expenditure on primary schools increased tenfold in money terms and doubled its share of total capital expenditure on education; total expenditure on primary education increased in real terms by 54 per cent between 1964 and 1974; real current expenditure per pupil increased 15 per cent in the period 1970–74; primary pupil–teacher ratios in England and Wales improved from 1:28.3 in 1965 to 1:24.7 in 1974 (according to Peston, 1979). Primary Education was the subject of three-year inquiries by the Central Advisory Councils for Education whose reports published in 1967 endorsed the curricular and pedagogic trends they detected and brought the sector into the political limelight. Building programmes, action research projects, the expansion of nursery education and of teacher training and the provision of extra allowances and resources in EPA areas all acknowledged the new priority being accorded the sector both by the Wilson administrations of 1964–70 and the succeeding Heath government whose White Paper, *A Framework for Expansion* (1972), promised 'to bring about a shift of resources within the education budget in favour of primary schools'. Characterized by post-Plowden euphoria, primary education was witnessing 'a golden age', even though in 1972 there was a disquietening report on reading standards (Start and Wells, 1972) and in December 1973 government expenditure cuts were announced by Antony Barber following a tremendous increase in world oil prices.

Though there were no startling educational events in 1974, a number of developments can be traced back to that year. It was the year when the Barber cuts began to have an impact, when local government was reorganized, when an announcement was made about the setting up of the Assessment of Performance Unit, when the feasibility study for the HMI primary survey was undertaken and when the

Houghton Report on teachers' pay was issued. In January 1974 Terry Ellis took up his headship at William Tyndale Junior School; in September the Bullock Report, recommending a system of monitoring, was submitted to the Secretary of State; and, in December, Burstall reported that following a large-scale evaluation study there was 'on balance' no case for the further extension of primary French (Burstall et al., 1974). It was also in 1974 when the number of primary children in England and Wales first fell from a peak the previous year, and when the Permanent Secretary at the Department of Education and Science 'wondered aloud' to an OECD examining panel 'whether the Government could continue to debar itself from what had been termed "the secret garden of the curriculum"'.

The period since 1974 could be presented in a variety of ways, each with its advantages and disadvantages. Instead of presenting a chronology of significant events or characterizing the period in terms of the activities of particular individuals, this chapter analyses developments in primary education in terms of four general topics — contraction, curriculum, pedagogy and evaluation. In relation to each topic, particular issues are identified, and selected events and persons in turn related briefly to these.

Contraction

In contrast to the expansion and optimism noted above, 'the educational story of the last few years is one of a retreat from optimism and a decline not only in the value placed upon education but also in the scale of the enterprise' (Bernbaum, 1979, pp. 1–2). Contraction provides the backdrop against which other educational developments have occurred. The long-term impact of contraction is impossible to determine but already it has had important repercussions for the education service in general and for primary education in particular. Even so, its significance has, arguably, not fully penetrated the consciousness of many practitioners whose frames of reference are still embedded in the expansive context of that 'golden age' before 1974. Contraction has taken, and continues to take, a variety of forms: *demographic, economic* and, more elusively, a contraction in *expectations*.

In terms of demography the primary school population in England and Wales reached a peak in 1973 when there were about $5^1/_4$ million children in maintained nursery and primary schools; by 1979, numbers had fallen by about half a million (Collings, 1980). During the period 1974–79 the total number of qualified teachers in English nursery and primary schools fell by almost 3,000 to 194,000, though the pupil–teacher ratio improved from 1:24.9 to 1:23.1, thus sustaining the improvement from 1965 already noted (DES, 1979b). This drop of half a million pupils coupled with central government and local authority policies has had a decimating effect on primary teacher training (Hencke, 1978); has resulted in considerable staff redeployment; and has caused the closure or amalgamation of a very considerable number of schools. Falling rolls have contributed to the disappearance of remedial teaching and other part-time provision in some schools; to a greater incidence of mixed-age classes; to a lessening of teacher mobility across local authority boundaries;

and to problems in covering an appropriate range of work in the curriculum (Thomas, 1980). Such difficulties are likely to be exacerbated in the next five years since a further fall of one million primary-aged pupils will occur in England and Wales by 1986. Of the 30 per cent decline in primary population between 1974 and 1986 only just over a third had affected schools by the beginning of 1980. Whereas policy-makers in the 1950s and 1960s were preoccupied by the problems of teacher supply and school building for a rapidly expanding population, those of the 1980s will be preoccupied with the still more difficult task of managing a contracting service. Any changes in curriculum, pedagogy, evaluation, organization development or educational research will take place against this backcloth.

The demographic turndown occurred at the same time as the rate of growth of most western economies declined sharply. The mid- and late 1970s were years of economic recession with a relative decline in world trade, large increases in rates of unemployment and, in the United Kingdom, an unusually high rate of domestic inflation. In Britain, big spending services such as education 'ground to a crawl as the hare of public expenditure was harnessed to the tortoise of economic growth' (MacDonald, 1979, p. 28). Pressures for greater cost-effectiveness grew stronger; politicians such as James Callaghan in his 1976 Ruskin College speech wondered whether the education service was giving value for money. In view of demographic trends and developing political disillusionment with education (referred to below) education budgets were tempting targets, especially in crisis years such as 1976 when a package of £6000 million public expenditure cuts was announced. It is, however, important to note that, comparing 1974–75 with 1978–79, central government's total current and capital expenditure on state schools fell less than is commonly supposed: there was a fall of £406 million in capital expenditure partly compensated by a rise of £319 million on current expenditure at 1979 survey prices. There were some major casualties: for example, capital expenditure for nursery education peaked at £46 million in 1975–76 and fell to less than £15 million in succeeding years. What *did* contract during this period was *planned* expenditure for the expansion of the education service. However, the four years from 1980 onwards certainly threatened more substantial 'real' cuts in government expenditure. Attention here has been focused on central government, but throughout the latter half of the 1970s local authorities, too, were instituting economies in the education service, partly because of pressure on their locally generated resources — as witnessed by successive cuts in capitation allowances in 'real' terms, cut-backs in inservice provision of various kinds and drastic reductions in ancillary services.

Less easy to characterize and to document is a third aspect of contraction — contraction in political, public and professional expectations of schooling. The following extract from an editorial written towards the end of 1974 provides the background to this disillusionment and illustrates the emergence of professional awareness of it:

In retrospect the period 1960–70 may well appear as a golden age for education. During that decade educational institutions were regarded as very important indeed, even vital to our future well-being as a nation. Expenditure on education rose rapidly; expansion was the order of the day; public interest grew greater and more informed. Education was claimed as a most important factor in promoting social equality, racial harmony, technological advance, economic prosperity, individual mental health. On both sides of the Atlantic, public funds were grasped eagerly in attempts to bring these claims to reality. Yet this reality has remained elusive; education has not produced startling changes in the wider society. With recent cut-backs in expenditure, reaction to ROSLA, fall-off in university applications and retrenchment in teacher education, could we be witnessing the beginnings of governmental and public disillusionment with educational institutions? If so, then part of the blame lies with those in education who have claimed too much, who have promised goods they couldn't possibly deliver, unaided by major social and economic changes in society. (Richards, 1975, p. 3)

By the mid-1970s, politicians had become highly sceptical about the relationship of educational investment to economic growth and about the socially equalizing effects of such investment. The grandiose claims of the 1960s were replaced in Callaghan's Ruskin College speech by more sober, pragmatic purposes: 'to equip children to the best of their ability for a lively, constructive place in society and also to fit them to do a job of work' (Callaghan, 1976). From viewing education as a social panacea — and primary education in particular as a major weapon against poverty — politicians became much more circumspect in their statements about education: a suspicion, even resentment, of being misled by educationists could be detected. It is less easy to document public and professional reactions: how far the former shared politicians' bold aspirations and consequent disillusionment is not clear, though there were certainly worries about educational standards. How far professionals shared the decline in expectations is not easy to discover. Undoubtedly, some were disillusioned that the education service had not fulfilled the social democratic ideals of the 1960s. All were caught up in the general unease and disillusion of a nation (and education system) in crisis and contraction. At national level the unbridled assertions of the previous decade were far less in evidence — both during the 'Great Debate' of 1977 and its aftermath. The heady idealism of Plowden gave way to the more circumspect, measured aspirations of the 1978 HMI primary survey. However, it has to be acknowledged that what some may applaud as realistic aspirations, others may regard as the colourless, sombre products of pragmatism and retrenchment.

Curriculum

For our purposes the curriculum can be regarded as comprising patterns of educa-tional experience or courses of study provided by teachers in primary schools. In the period 1974–80, the primary curriculum was an area of ideological conflict and a number of issues in particular became the centre of attention: *range, structure, appropriateness, consistency* and *continuity*. Such conflict was inevitable in a demo-cratic society. The curriculum is a vehicle for introducing children to valued skills, predispositions, interests, concepts, attitudes and substantive knowledge. 'Valued' is a most significant adjective: within our society and its teaching profession there is disagreement over what is 'valuable' and the curriculum inevitably reflects that conflict. As Alan Blyth remarked, 'Everybody agrees that curriculum matters. That is probably the extent of agreement about curriculum' (Blyth, 1978, p. 25). Throughout the 1970s the primary curriculum and primary pedagogy were the foci of ideological conflict. At least four major ideologies could be identified (Richards, 1979, p. 41):

a) *'liberal romanticism'* — celebrating the supremacy of the child in the teaching–learning situation and regarding the curriculum as the sum total of learning experiences both offered to them and created by them as they interact with their surroundings.

b) *'educational conservatism'* — stressing the importance of continuity with the past and the curriculum as the repository of worthwhile cultural elements which need transmitting from one generation to another.

c) *'liberal pragmatism'* — holding an increasingly influential middle ground position, viewing the curriculum as a set of learning experiences largely but not entirely structured by the teacher, but respecting to some degree both the individuality of the child and the importance of cultural transmission.

d) *'social democracy'* — viewing the curriculum as a means towards realizing social justice and focused around the social experience of pupils.

Discussion as to the purposes of the primary curriculum continued throughout the 1970s — stimulated by empirical data from the Aims of Primary Education project (Ashton et al., 1975); given sharper, more urgent focus by Auld's castigation of the ILEA for having no policy 'as to the aims and objectives of the primary curriculum being provided in its schools' (Auld, 1976); and carried further by DES publications since the 'Great Debate'. In particular, from 1976, Her Majesty's Inspectorate took a public lead on curriculum matters based on developing and clarifying a professional consensus. How far such a consensus is possible among conflicting ideological interest groups is a question which may be answered in the 1980s.

The *range* of the primary curriculum was a continuing issue from 1974 onwards. There were some moves towards its narrowing. Alarmingly readable, Black Paper writings (for example, Boyson, 1975; Cox and Boyson, 1975, 1977) reasserted the need for concentration on the 'basics' (usually interpreted as reading, writing and ciphering), albeit sometimes with concessions to a minimum body of scientific, historical, geographical and religious knowledge. There was a growing consensus that primary French was best excluded unless capable staff, adequate resources and a substantial degree of curriculum continuity could be assured. On the other hand, there was increasing advocacy of the place of science — as witnessed by the HMI primary survey and Schools Council initiatives. The former argued that, with the inclusion of science, 'the curriculum is probably wide enough to serve current educational needs' (DES, 1978, p. 126). Hard evidence, publicly available, about the range of the curriculum was almost non-existent. The primary survey did provide evidence as to the extent to which certain curriculum items appeared in the classes inspected, but no overall analysis of the range of the primary curriculum was published. Lack of comprehensive information remains a major shortcoming in professional and public discussion of curriculum range.

Between 1974 and 1980 there was major concern over the issue of *structure* in the primary curriculum, though compared with complaints about its absence there were far fewer attempts to spell out what this 'structure' might be. In this connection, Bennett was an important opinion former. Following his attempted evaluation of the relationship between teaching styles and pupil progress he suggested that 'careful and clear structuring of activities together with a curriculum which emphasizes cognitive content are the keys to enhanced academic progress' (Bennett et al., 1976, p. 160), but provided no analysis of what that structuring entailed. Lack of structure was a prominent slogan in the war-cries of Black Paper critics. Only occasionally did such critics argue their case through: one such was Bantock who criticized the approach of the modern British primary school 'in its more progressive guise' for failing 'to convey the structures of knowledge in a coherent fashion' thereby fostering 'a magpie curriculum of bits and pieces, unrelated and ephemeral' (Bantock, 1980, p. 44). This concern over possible fragmentation and trivialization of the curriculum was echoed, in part at least, by HMI criticisms of the topic approach where they noted a danger of both fragmentation and repetition unless teachers were very clear of the ideas, skills and techniques that children might learn as they progressed through primary school (Thomas, 1980). Unlike Bantock and the Inspectorate, too many people equated 'structure' with organized instruction in the 'basics'. Recent work on primary science (for example, Harlen, 1978, 1980b), the social subjects (Blyth et al., 1976) and mathematics (DES, 1979a) has gone some way to spelling out skills, concepts, principles and generalizations, in this way providing tentative structures to various areas of knowledge in relation to which schools might plan and sequence the learning experiences offered to pupils.

The *appropriateness* of the curriculum is a perennial question, though professional discussion of the form of its supposed inappropriateness tended to shift from the early to the late 1970s. Throughout the period, 'child-centred' educationists argued that the curriculum experienced by many children was inappropriate to their 'needs' and 'interests'. In the early 1970s, 'needs' and 'interests' were also invoked by community-centred advocates such as Midwinter (1972) who accused most urban schools of failing to provide a curriculum which connected with the local community context and which helped children respond creatively to the challenge of living in disadvantaged areas. Both such views were less publicly in evidence by the end of the decade when a different form of inappropriateness was being highlighted. According to the primary survey there was considerable mismatch between the capacities of the children and the work they were being given; this mismatch being particularly marked in the case of abler compared with average and below-average pupils, and older compared with younger pupils. Discussion of this ability-linked inappropriateness was accompanied by an increasing concern for suitably providing for the 'gifted': much effort went into identifying such children, less into providing suitable material and teaching strategies. One other recent development needs noting, though it has yet to develop a substantial public or professional voice. It is being argued that current suggestions for rendering the primary curriculum more appropriate have completely failed to take cognizance of the 'information and knowledge revolution' that is already upon us.

Lastly, *consistency* and *continuity* are two related concepts referring to issues of increasing importance in curricular discussion. Curriculum consistency is a 'horizontal' concept referring to the extent to which all pupils at a particular stage, whether in the same class or different classes, are introduced to a similar set of curricular elements. References to a core curriculum (as in the Yellow Book prepared for the Prime Minister by the DES in 1976), to a 'protected part of the curriculum' (in the 1977 Green Paper), and to 'a framework for the school curriculum' (DES, 1980) involved consideration of the degree of curriculum consistency believed appropriate for English and Welsh schools, primary as well as secondary. Recent government thinking is crystallized in a statement from *A Framework for the School Curriculum*: 'The Secretaries of State consider that the diversity of practice that has emerged in recent years, as shown particularly by HM Inspectors' national surveys of primary and secondary schools, makes it timely to prepare guidance on the place which certain key elements in the curriculum should have in the experience of every pupil during the compulsory period of education' (DES, 1980, p. 5).

Curriculum continuity is a 'vertical' concept referring to the extent to which curricular experiences offered to pupils relate to, and build on, those offered previously. Continuity can refer to the transition pupils experience between primary and secondary stages, to intra-school transition as children move from class to class, and to continuity of experience within any one class during the course of a school year. The key question here was posed by Sheila Browne: 'How far and in what ways is continuity essential to a valid curriculum?' (1977, p. 37). After the 1944 Act established primary and secondary stages of education, lip-service was paid to the notion of inter-stage continuity, but it was only in the 1970s with the widespread incidence of comprehensive secondary education (and three-tier systems in particular) that the problem of continuity was highlighted. The primary survey commented that 'the importance of continuity in the curriculum of the (contributory and receiving) schools was largely overlooked' (p. 39); the wider adoption of primary French was discouraged partly for the same reason; and many curriculum projects cutting across stages (for example, Science 5–13) did not make much impact in overcoming the divide at 11 years. Intra-school continuity is becoming increasingly recognized as a major problem: local authority guidelines, curriculum review documents and renewed attention to record-keeping are all illustrative of a growing concern for the continuity of children's experience within schools. Both curriculum consistency and continuity, however, raise a number of difficult professional issues concerned with teacher autonomy, curriculum planning and implementation, school policy-making, and local and national responsibilities for curriculum decision-making — all issues raised in the government's revised framework document *The School Curriculum* (DES, 1981).

Pedagogy

By pedagogy is meant that complex of teaching approaches, skills, strategies, tactics and forms of organization through which the curriculum is transacted by teachers and pupils. Like the primary curriculum, pedagogy was the subject of considerable controversy but, compared with the curriculum, a smaller number of developments could be discerned.

The most obvious of these, both to the teaching profession and the general public, was the virulent criticism of so-called 'informal', 'modern' or 'progressive' methods which gathered force from 1969 onwards. There is little doubt that the Plowden Report of 1967 marked the acceptance of 'child-centred' ideology as the orthodoxy of primary education, at least as perceived by many policy-makers, commentators and educationists. That it was ever so regarded by the majority of teachers is much more questionable. Plowden gave a general endorsement to methods of teaching which were less directive than those presumed to have characterized elementary education and its post-1944 counterpart. Plowden found it impossible to characterize these less directive methods succinctly or unambiguously; others since, except the most extreme critics, have found it equally difficult (see Bennett et al., 1976, Galton et al., 1980). But within eight years of Plowden's publication criticisms of these methods were widely publicized in the media — fuelled initially by Black Paper polemicists who, alone, had no difficulty in characterizing them — as based on the belief that 'children should not be told anything but must find out for themselves' (Cox and Dyson, 1969).

Criticism reached a peak in 1976 with the publication of Bennett's *Teaching Styles and Pupil Progress*; the Auld Inquiry into the William Tyndale Junior School (where, it appeared, 'progressive methods' had been taken to an extreme); and the leaked observations of the Inspectorate about the use of the child-centred approach in the hands of less able or inexperienced teachers. Indeed, 1976 was a particularly significant date in the pedagogic debate of the 1970s. It is important to note that prior to that time no detailed characterization of teaching methods ('modern' or otherwise) in English primary schools had been put forward; there had been very little evidence as to the incidence of different methods and, with the exception of a study by Gardner (1966), no large-scale, reasonably comprehensive assessment of their effectiveness in terms of pupil performance had been attempted. From 1976 onwards, *attempts* were made to place pedagogic debate on a sounder conceptual and empirical base.

The word 'attempts' needs stressing, since the phenomena under investigation are very complex (whether considered theoretically or practically) and the systematic study of primary pedagogy is in its early infancy. Bennett himself attempted to capture something of this complexity by deriving twelve inadequately characterized 'teaching styles' from a cluster analysis of junior teachers' questionnaire responses. A similarly inadequate categorization was employed in the primary survey which postulated two broad approaches to teaching: 'mainly didactic' and 'mainly exploratory'. Recently the Observational Research and Classroom Learning Evaluation (ORACLE) project attempted a more rigorous analysis, distinguishing between teaching strategies (organizational, curricular and instructional) and sets of teaching tactics which it termed 'styles'. Based on cluster analysis of data provided by systematic classroom observation (not questionnaire responses), three 'primary' teaching styles were derived; a fourth was less clearly delineated and seemed more accurately described as a 'secondary' style comprising varied mixtures of the three 'primary' ones. Though still crude compared with pedagogic phenomena such 'styles' were more easily recognizable, more firmly based on observational data and less simplistic than those employed by Bennett, by the HMI primary survey and by Black Paper polemicists.

Empirical research made a second important contribution to pedagogic debate. The studies quoted above — along with others by Bealing (1972), Ashton et al. (1975) and Bassey (1978) — helped defuse the explosive notion of 'a primary school revolution' along progressive lines. The incidence of such practices, however defined, was revealed as far less than either the advocates or the detractors of 'child-centred' ideology maintained. Only one fifth of ORACLE's teachers (of junior-aged children) adopted a heavily individualized teaching approach, only a tenth of Bennett's sample reported having a teaching style which the researchers believed corresponded to 'the Plowden definition' and less than one teacher in twenty relied mainly on an 'exploratory' approach when inspected as part of the primary survey. The rabid progressives, much castigated by Black Paper writers, had either left teaching, had reverted to less extreme pedagogic forms or, most probably, had never existed in significant numbers.

A third related development was a more considered attempt to assess the differential effects of teaching approaches on pupil attainment. It was this aspect of Bennett's work which helped bring criticism of primary education to a peak in 1976. Compared with research on similar areas in the United States, his findings, and the way in which they were presented, were strikingly unequivocal: 'The effect of teaching style is statistically and educationally significant in all attainment areas tested. The analysis shows clearly the general efficacy of formal methods in the basic subjects.' HMI's analysis presented a different picture. In the primary survey, in classes where a combination of exploratory and didactic approaches were used, children scored higher on NFER tests in reading and mathematics compared with classes where only one approach was mainly used. (However, these scores were only significantly higher when compared with classes taught mainly by exploratory methods.) Compared with previous studies the ORACLE project attempted to widen the basis of pupil attainment to include study skills (strangely characterized), listening skills and skills in acquiring information other than by reading. Their findings suggested that overall 'no single approach can claim to have a monopoly of desirable characteristics', though two particular styles came out best in the 'league tables' which the researchers obligingly, but misguidedly, provided. Such findings are unlikely to be accepted as definitive and strengthen, rather than weaken, arguments for much more sophisticated assessment techniques and much more sophisticated conceptualizations of primary school pedagogy. The pedagogic debate will undoubtedly continue in the 1980s.

Evaluation

The period 1974–80 was also characterized by demands for better, more publicly accessible appraisals of aspects of schooling and for greater accountability of teachers and the education service to the community at large. Such demands were often made in the context of a concern for 'standards' — though the meaning of this term and the particular aspects of schooling to which it was being applied were often unclear. Neither did clarity or precision characterize discussion within the professional community, so obscuring information and making a response to public demands more difficult.

A wide definition of evaluation is adopted here and related both to other concepts and to actual developments during the period. Following Harlen, evaluation is taken to comprise 'not only the collection of information but the identification and use of criteria for making judgements about the information . . . Assessment is just one way of gathering information, which involves some attempt at measurement' (Harlen, 1980a). With these distinctions in mind the demand for teacher accountability becomes an assertion that teachers are obliged to provide an account of their activities based on carefully collected information and on related judgments made in relation to explicit criteria. Two forms of accountability can be distinguished (Sockett, 1980): accountability for outcomes and results of schooling (product accountability); and accountability in terms of adherence to professional standards of integrity and practice (process accountability).

One major mode of response underpinned by a product model of accountability was to introduce more widespread assessment procedures to collect information about pupil performance. Demands for better, more regular assessment nationwide gathered strength with the publication of the Bullock Report in 1975, whose first major recommendation was that 'a system of monitoring should be introduced which will employ new instruments to assess a wider range of attainments than has been attempted in the past and allow new criteria to be established for the definition of literacy' (DES, 1975, p. 513). Work was already in hand to produce tests of attainment in mathematics and, in the previous year, the DES had announced the establishment of the Assessment of Performance Unit to develop methods of assessing and monitoring, over time, the achievements of children at school. The APU became an established part of the educational scene in the late 1970s and began to monitor the performance of primary pupils in language, mathematics and science. Its establishment stimulated less opposition from teachers than from educationists. Some of the latter, for example, accused it of attempting to establish bureaucratic rather than professional control over schooling and criticized its assessment structure as 'technocratic in form, determinist in values and precariously dependent upon a costly and defect-ridden technology of test construction' (MacDonald, 1979). Parallel with the activities of the APU was the introduction of testing in a large number of LEAs (for example, Croydon, Redbridge, Hillingdon, Birmingham, Lancashire) to see how well schools were performing in terms of measurable pupil outcomes. An alternative mode underpinned by a process model of accountability involved gathering descriptive data in school settings about events, conditions, activities and performances (teachers' as well as pupils') and comparing these against descriptive criteria in the form of schedules or checklists. Some local authorities renamed their advisers 'inspectors' and stepped up the number of inspections as a way of evaluating professional performance. Some (for example, ILEA, Oxfordshire) involved teachers in devising self-appraisal schedules to assist staff in the clarification of objectives and priorities and in the identification of strengths and weaknesses. Curriculum guidelines were widely produced to assist curriculum planning, implementation and evaluation.

The two major modes of response were not mutually exclusive, as illustrated by the HMI primary survey which conducted an appraisal using quantitative and qualitative data. Testing some pupils' performances in reading and mathematics was undertaken but the test data were only complementary to a much greater mass of qualitative data gathered in relation to detailed schedules during inspections. The report was the first publicly accessible, overall evaluation of primary education in England containing information and judgments and revealing some of the criteria used in the making of such judgments. Developments outlined above were, in part at least, responses to public concern over 'standards' — originally articulated by the Black Papers and fuelled in the mid-1970s by the Tyndale affair, politicians, journalists and, to some extent, employers. The education service's utilization of both major modes of response will, in future, provide empirical data (both descriptive and numerical) as to levels of attainment reached by pupils and schools — one sense of the term 'standards'. But neither mode will be able to resolve the issue of 'standards' in its second sense, that is, levels of competence which *should* be reached (Straughan and Wrigley, 1980). Such a value-laden issue will undoubtedly, inevitably and rightly continue to be debated through the 1980s, irrespective of what methods of evaluation or models of accountability are operative in schools.

Conclusion: The Issue of Control

Primary school curriculum, pedagogy and evaluation have been considered and set in a context of contraction. But contraction itself is only part of the wider social context where the problem of social control is a dominant one. Many commentators (for example, MacLure, 1979; Lynch, 1980) would agree with MacDonald (1979) that pressures on the education service during the mid- and late 1970s were symptomatic of the 'malaise of liberal democracy ... in a society believed to be in decline and out of legitimate control'. Arguably, as the most readily accessible of all social services, schools received the brunt of public dissatisfaction with the welfare state which had spawned an increasingly remote and proliferated bureaucracy and had been unable to satisfy growing demands for much higher living standards and for greater social justice. Certainly, from 1974, the education service witnessed attempts at reasserting democratic control over its activities — through politicians bringing the curriculum back into the public arena; through more interventionist policies by local authority corporate managers and elected members;

through the rediscovery by some school governors of their powers and responsibilities under the 1944 Act; and through parental pressures for greater information about schools and for participation on governing bodies (acknowledged by the Taylor Report of 1977 and implemented in part by the 1980 Education Act).

Up till the present, power over English primary schools has been both partial and distributed: central government (through the DES), local authorities, teachers and, to a smaller extent, the local community have shared in it, but no one party has been able unilaterally to impose its will on the others. Since 1974 the myth of unbridled teacher autonomy over curriculum, pedagogy and evaluation has been exposed, though the necessity (let alone desirability) of some scope for autonomous decision-making by teachers remains. From time to time assertions have been made about government intentions to impose centralized control of schools. At the present time it is not at all clear whether greater leadership and coordination from the centre, extended policy-making and management by local authorities and greater community participation at local levels are producing a change in the distribution of power. Certainly, the delicate, intricate balance which has evolved since 1944 will not change overnight. Perhaps the *Times Educational Supplement* was right in predicting a long and shuffling process of readjustment between all parties concerned, with the DES and local authorities likely to gain most in terms of increased leverage (though not finely detailed control) over the system. The future is uncertain. The golden age of the 1960s is unlikely to be echoed by a 1980s equivalent but the issues raised have still to be worked through. There will be challenges enough related to influence and control, contraction, policy-making, evaluation, accountability, professional development and research as well as the implications of the 'information revolution' already upon us. Meeting such challenges will not be comfortable nor easy but neither will it be boring or lacklustre.

References

ASHTON, P., KNEN, P. and DAVIES, F. (1975) *The Aims of Primary Education: A Study of Teachers' Opinions*, London: Macmillan Education.

AULD, R. (1976) *William Tyndale Junior and Infants Schools Public Inquiry*, London: ILEA.

BANTOCK, G. (1980) *Dilemmas of the Curriculum*, Oxford: Martin Robertson.

BASSEY, M. (1978) *Nine Hundred Primary School Teachers*, Slough: NFER.

BEALING, D. (1972) 'The organization of junior school classrooms', *Education Research*, **14**, 3, pp. 231–5.

BENNETT, S.N. with JORDAN, J., LONG, G. and WADE, B. (1976) *Teaching Styles and Pupil Progress*, London: Open Books.

BERNBAUM, G. (ed.) (1979) *Schooling in Decline*, London: Macmillan.

BLYTH, W. (1978) 'The curriculum in the middle years', *Education 3–13*, **6**, 2.

BLYTH, W. with COOPER, K., DERRICOTT, R., ELLIOTT, G., SUMMER, H. and WAPLINGTON, A. (1976) *Place, Time and Society 8–13: Curriculum Planning in History, Geography and Social Science*, Glasgow: Collins.

BOYSON, R. (1975) 'Maps, chaps and your hundred best books', *Times Educational Supplement*, 17 October.

BROWNE, S. (1977) 'Curriculum: An HMI view' *Trends in Education*, Autumn.

BURSTALL, C., JAMIESON, M., COHEN, C. and HARGREAVES, M. (1974) *Primary French in the Balance*, Slough: NFER.

CENTRAL ADVISORY COUNCIL FOR EDUCATION (England) (1967) *Children and Their Primary Schools* (The Plowden Report), London: HMSO.

CALLAGHAN, J. (1976) 'Towards a national debate' (The Ruskin College speech), *Education*, 22 October.

COLLINGS, H. (1980) 'Falling rolls', in RICHARDS, C. (ed.) *Primary Education: Issues for the Eighties*, London: A. and C. Black.

COX, C. and BOYSON, R. (eds) (1975) *Black Paper 1975*, London: Dent.

COX, C. and BOYSON, R. (eds) (1977) *Black Paper 1977*, London: Temple Smith.

COX, C. and DYSON, T. (eds) (1969) *Fight for Education*, London: Critical Quarterly Society.

DEPARTMENT OF EDUCATION AND SCIENCE (1975) *A Language for Life* (The Bullock Report), London: HMSO.

DEPARTMENT OF EDUCATION AND SCIENCE (1977a) *Education in Schools: A Consultative Document* (The Green Paper), London: HMSO.

DEPARTMENT OF EDUCATION AND SCIENCE/WELSH OFFICE (1977b) *A New Partnership for Our Schools* (The Taylor Report), London: HMSO.

DEPARTMENT OF EDUCATION AND SCIENCE (1978) *Primary Education in England: A Survey by HM Inspectors of Schools*, London: HMSO.

DEPARTMENT OF EDUCATION AND SCIENCE (1979a) *Mathematics 5–11*, HMI Series: Matters for Discussion 9, London: HMSO.

DEPARTMENT OF EDUCATION AND SCIENCE (1979b) *Statistical Bulletin 17/79*, London: HMSO.

DEPARTMENT OF EDUCATION AND SCIENCE/WELSH OFFICE (1980) *A Framework for the School Curriculum*, London: DES.

DEPARTMENT OF EDUCATION AND SCIENCE/WELSH OFFICE (1981) *The School Curriculum*, London: HMSO.

GALTON, M., SIMON, B. and CROLL, P. (1980) *Inside the Primary Classroom*, London: Routledge and Kegan Paul.

GARDNER, D. (1966) *Experiment and Tradition in Primary Schools*, London: Methuen.

HARLEN, W. (1978) 'Does content matter in primary science?', *School Science Review*, 209.

HARLEN, W. (1980a) 'Evaluation in education', in STRAUGHAN, R. and WRIGLEY, J. (eds) *Values and Evaluation in Education*, London: Harper and Row.

HARLEN, W. (1980b) 'Selecting content in primary science', *Education 3–13*, **8**, 2.

HENCKE, D. (1978) *Colleges in Crisis: The Reorganisation of Teacher Training 1971–77*, Harmondsworth: Penguin.

LYNCH, J. (1980) 'Legitimation crisis for the English middle school', in HARGREAVES, A. and TICKLE, L. (eds) *Middle Schools: Origins, Ideology and Practice*, London: Harper and Row.

MACDONALD, B. (1979) 'Hard times: Educational accountability in England', *Educational Analysis*, **1**, 1.

MACLURE, S. (1979) 'The endless agenda: Matters arising', *Oxford Review of Education*, **5**, 2.

MIDWINTER, E. (1972) *Priority Education*, Harmondsworth: Penguin.

NATIONAL UNION OF TEACHERS (1979) *The Cost of the Cuts*, London: NUT.

PESTON, M. (1979) 'United Kingdom (England and Wales)', in *Educational Financing and Policy Goals for Primary Schools, Country Reports, Volume II United Kingdom, United States, Yugoslavia*, Paris, OECD.

RICHARD, C. (1975) 'Claims', *Education 3–13*, **3**, 1.

RICHARDS, C. (1979) 'Primary education: Myth, belief and practice', in BLOOMER, M. and SHAW, K. (eds) *The Challenge of Educational Change*, Oxford: Pergamon.

SOCKETT, H. (ed.) (1980) *Accountability in the English Educational System*, London: Hodder and Stoughton.

START, K. and WELLS, B. (1972) *The Trend of Reading Standards*, Slough: NFER.

STRAUGHAN, R. and WRIGLEY, J. (eds) (1980) *Values and Evaluation in Education*, London: Harper and Row.

THOMAS, N. (1980) 'The primary curriculum: Survey findings and implications', in RICHARDS, C. (ed.) *Primary Education: Issues for the Eighties*, London: A. and C. Black.

WHITE PAPER (1972) *Education: A Framework for Expansion* (Cmnd. 5174), London: HMSO.

4 The 'Primary School Revolution' Demythologized — An Appraisal of the HMI Primary Survey

More than other sectors of the education system, primary education seems subject to myth-making. Myths can be positive and supportive; they may be negative and condemnatory. A myth associated with the Plowden Report and very much in currency in the early 1970s was of an 'educational revolution' along child-centred lines. It still lingers on 25 years later — reasserted by right-wing critics whose knowledge of the state education system is at best second- or even third-hand. That 'revolution', redolent of the expansionist, optimistic 1960s, was believed by the writers of the Plowden Report to represent 'a quickening trend' which promised to transform primary education. It never happened, though it did provide inspiration for some teachers and frustration and disbelief for others (myself included) who could not understand how the tenets of what passed for child-centred education could be applied to their classes without resulting in near-anarchy and chaos. But a fascinating puzzle remains: how, where and why did the myth originate and who perpetuated it and benefited from its dissemination?

As this chapter, written in 1979, argues, the debunking of the myth was accomplished primarily by the national survey of English primary education carried out by HMI and published in 1978 under the title Primary Education in England: A Survey by HM Inspectors of Schools. *This provided firm evidence of curricular and pedagogic continuities between pre- and post-Plowden practice in the vast majority of schools. It showed that with the advent of non-streaming and the spread of mixed-ability classes organizational changes had occurred. There was more individual and group teaching than previously and there were changes in the ways in which classes were organized and in the layout of classrooms, but the curriculum was 'scarcely more than a revamped elementary school curriculum with the same major utilitarian emphases' (an equally apt description of the current post-1997 ITEMS — IT, English, mathematics and science — curriculum). The primary survey was important as a rigorous professional appraisal of post-Plowden primary education and as an agenda-setting publication which provided the impetus for a decade of HMI-led initiatives in primary education.*

When the history of English primary education in the twentieth century comes to be written, three dates are likely to be seen as particularly significant: 1931, when the notion of the 'primary school' received official recognition in the Hadow Report;

1967, when 'child-centred education' (however loosely defined) was accepted as the official orthodoxy of English primary education; and 1978, when the publication of *Primary Education in England: A Survey by HM Inspectors of Schools* provided the first publicly accessible, rigorous overall appraisal since Hadow. (The appraisal conducted by the Inspectors for the Plowden Committee in the 1960s did not, in my view, meet these criteria.) The survey published in 1978 counters very effectively the wild assertions and scaremongering rife following Tyndale and Bennett in 1976 — a year when the fortunes of primary education reached their nadir. However, it provided cold comfort for curriculum developers and for both the advocates and the critics of 'child-centred education'. To my mind, with the major exception of its very simplistic treatment of teaching approaches, the survey does justice to many of the complexities, successes, short-comings and subtleties of primary practice.

The survey's findings and recommendations do not rest on carefully conducted classroom observational research. It is an evaluation report in a very important but (for curriculum workers) much neglected tradition which has its own repertoire of techniques, its own standards of appraisal and its own code of professional conduct — a tradition stemming from the 'craft' of school inspection. However, the confidential, almost apostolic, nature of the transmission of this craft (itself predating curriculum evaluation as we know it by almost a century) makes it impossible for outsiders to provide (in its own terms) methodological critiques of the national inspection reported in the survey. Perhaps publication of this and other recent DES appraisals of practice might encourage curriculum scholars interested in evaluation to explore more thoroughly the problems and issues raised by the evaluative aspects of inspection.

Most importantly, the survey underlines the centrality of the curriculum in primary education. Its concern for intellectual development through appropriately designed curricula represents a significant readjustment of emphasis compared with Plowden; though important, organization, pupil grouping, teaching approaches, staffing and resource allocation have for too long preoccupied decision-makers in primary schools and deflected them from the still more central tasks of deciding what particular skills, concepts, knowledge and attitudes primary children should acquire and of incorporating these into planned (and evaluated) teaching/learning sequences. The report focuses on these problems, draws up a valuable, though incomplete, agenda for professional discussion (which cannot be reviewed in detail here) and provides opportunities for work in curriculum studies to make a contribution to reviewing, refining and enhancing the rather impoverished primary curriculum.

Curriculum studies in the British tradition have been largely ameliorative in orientation, with the problems of secondary education being predominant among its concerns. In comparison, the primary curriculum has been relatively neglected, partly at least because those working in curriculum have appeared to accept the mythology of primary education current over the last decade or so. The survey does much to 'demythologize' primary education. Judging from the practices revealed in the survey, the 'quickening trend' towards 'child-centred education' detected by the Plowden Committee has not materialized on a substantial scale in top infant and junior classes; 'the primary school revolution' has not been tried and found wanting but never been tried at all except in a small number of schools; most primary school teachers have not responded in the 'open', flexible, imaginative way curriculum developers assumed they would. In particular, most proposals for curriculum change made in the 1960s and early 1970s have been based on assumptions about teaching, learning, knowledge and children which do not appear to inform the practice of the majority of teachers. The current curriculum is revealed as scarcely more than a revamped elementary school curriculum with the same major utilitarian emphases.

These findings raise a number of interesting questions. How and why did the myth of 'the primary school revolution' arise? How was it sustained for such a long period? In whose interests was it perpetuated? What part was played in this by the media (and those with ready access to the media) and by individuals such as Christian Schiller who seems to have exercised an unpublicized but tremendous influence on many who later became important opinion-leaders? During the period 1960–75 what was the nature of the 'political' interplay among various interest groups within primary education? The major changes that the survey notes are organizational rather than curricular — in particular, the remarkable spread of non-streaming and the introduction of vertical grouping in a substantial number of infant and junior classrooms. How did the non-streaming movement develop, by whom was it fostered and for what reasons? Were the practices associated with the supposed 'revolution' simply teachers' pragmatic, relatively superficial responses to the need to cope with unstreamed or vertically grouped classes? Has organizational rather than curricular or pedagogic change been the major distinguishing feature of primary education during the last 20 years?

In this way, the publication of the national survey raises many important issues for students of the primary curriculum, some concerned with the recent history of primary education, and others with future curriculum policy-making (though the latter need the perspective provided by the former). The survey should be read as both an educational and a political document — political in the sense that it reflects and influences the distribution and exercise of power over the primary curriculum. If it appears to read awkwardly at times, this is not usually because it is hiding a lack of substance behind convoluted civil service prose. This is because it is deliberately conveying different messages at different levels to a variety of interest groups within and outside primary education. *Primary Education in England* is often very subtle and not always clear, but so is the process of primary education itself.

5   Primary Education 1980–87: An Analysis of Changes and Trends

The period 1980–87 was the end of an era. In retrospect it marked the end of central government's 'hands-off' policy in relation to LEAs and schools, the end of unfettered teacher autonomy and the end of all hope (for a decade at least) of re-establishing the growth in education that had characterized so much of the post-war period. Contraction and retrenchment were the order of the day as public spending on the social services (including education) became the focus for recurrent financial cuts and increasing political criticism. Step-by-step, circular-by-circular the government regulated the system, reined back LEAs and set the agenda for the education service. Unlike in the mid-1970s, primary education was not singled out for particular criticism or regulation though it shared in the ever-more stringent economic/political climate; and the contraction in pupil numbers hit it first and hardest and led to widespread personal and institutional insecurities. It was a time of increasing industrial tension and strife within the education service — around the middle of the decade the Thatcher Government took on both the miners and the teachers and imposed its will in both cases. Looking back, the move towards increasing central control was the necessary concomitant of the government's concern to destroy the 'nanny state' and replace it by a market-led, client-oriented economy regulated from the centre but providing opportunities for individual and corporate entrepreneurship in the interests of greater efficiency, effectiveness and competition. The transition from 'welfare state' to 'opportunity state' was a painful one, especially for those, including most teachers, whose professional assumptions had been forged in a very different climate. This chapter, written in 1987 just before the development of the National Curriculum, documents these changes.

Challenge

Children in primary schools grow physically at a fairly rapid rate; this physical growth is marked and incontrovertible. During their time in primary school, they develop intellectually, socially and emotionally; this development is not so clear cut nor as easily recognizable as physical growth but is real enough in the vast majority of cases. Partly because of teachers' close association and identification with young children, notions of growth and 'development' have been very much part of professional thinking in, and about, primary education itself. The assumption of growth and development in school children has been complemented by parallel assumptions of growth and development in the primary sector of education.

Very occasionally, children's physical development is markedly stunted and medical action is required; in a minority of cases, their intellectual development is considerably retarded and remediation is necessary, but for the most part, professional assumptions about children's growth are not seriously challenged. However, since the mid-1970s, professional assumptions of growth in primary education *have* been challenged. As an enterprise, primary education has not continued to grow, child-like; its growth, in terms of numbers of pupils and teachers, has been arrested, in some senses even reversed. Whether, as a result, its development as an enterprise has stagnated or regressed is more problematic and thus controversial. The underlying argument in this paper is that development has continued and continues.

Professional assumptions rest partly on close identification with children, but also in part from experience of living through periods of time with their own particular configurations of circumstances. The sense of loss and unease felt by many teachers in primary education during the last decade results from a challenge to their assumptions forged during a unique period of time (1944–74) when all of them were children in primary schools, teachers in primary schools or, in many cases, both. Two quotations from MacLure's book on the work of school architects, *Educational Development and School Building* (1984), provide pointers to current attitudes. The first provides a broad-brush picture of the first 25 years of post-war education:

> The period was one of unparalleled expansion in England and Wales. For a quarter of a century after the end of the Second World War, the social, economic and demographic conditions were uniquely favourable for educational development. It began with a strong political consensus behind the new Education Act which raised expectations and promised wider opportunities for everyone. On this basis, the education system was reconstructed and modernized . . . the consensus did not last: it crumbled in the 1960s, about the time the demographic trend turned down. The optimism and the expectations faded with the onset of a recession which ended the longest period of sustained prosperity the modern world has known. (p. ix)

It is important to note MacLure's words: '*unparalleled* expansion', 'conditions *uniquely* favourable', 'the *longest* period of *sustained* prosperity'. For those currently involved as teachers or advisers in primary education, their formative years in a professional sense occurred in a period which was economically and educationally aberrant. The loss of morale, which has characterized primary education, though not all primary schools, over the last decade (but particularly from 1980 to 1987) has arisen partly through the straightened circumstances of the time but partly from the atypicality of the previous period to which so many teachers have been, and to some extent still are, unwitting prisoners. In a second quotation, MacLure refers to changes in attitudes, thinking and practice required of school architects post-1975, once the period of unparalleled expansion had come to an end:

> To move out of the familiar thoughtforms of expansion and into the more austere disciplines of contraction and to do so creatively was by no means impossible but it called for a major effort of the imagination as well as a careful review of progress. (p. 265)

As far as primary teachers are concerned, the period since 1974 has witnessed considerable self-examination as the results of successive national surveys by HM Inspectorate have revealed the extent of the gap (inevitable to some degree) between aspiration and realization, between rhetoric and reality — soul-searching further promoted by local education authority curricular reviews and school self-evaluation activities. In some cases, unprofitable nostalgia has been the only result of such experiences. However, in others, realization of shortcomings has led to determination to tackle issues through policy formulation and implementation at national, local authority and school levels. Sometimes as a result of such initiatives and sometimes independent of them, many schools have continued to develop their conception of an appropriate primary education and have adapted to changing circumstances through the exercise of professional intelligence and imagination. Such schools have risen to the challenge presented by MacLure: development has continued despite, or in some cases even, spurred on by 'the more austere disciplines of contraction'.

The Wider Context

Issues in English primary education in the 1980s, the particular focus of this paper, need to be set in a wider temporal and geographical context if their significance is to be properly gauged. During the last two decades, a number of interconnected factors (demographic/cultural/economic/technological) have helped shape Western European societies and have, in turn, influenced provision and response in primary education. They have made it more difficult for primary education to pursue and fulfill its long-established purposes; more significantly still, they have made it necessary for those involved in primary education to review these purposes; to seek what elements of provision need to be reaffirmed, which redefined and which down-played, and to review the means through which purposes are enacted and elements provided. This process has been a Western European phenomenon, not unique in its scale or intensity to England.

Demographic changes result from the complex interplay among economic, social and cultural trends and the decisions of many millions of people. The most significant feature of the demographic situation in Western Europe has been the sharp decline in the number of births since 1965 — a decline which began to affect the number of children in primary schools during the 1970s. Countries suffered differentially from decline in primary school populations: some states such as the Federal Republic of West Germany and Austria experienced a 30 per cent fall from 1970 to 1982; others such as the United Kingdom, 20 per cent; and others such as Denmark and Norway less than 10 per cent. Although exact international figures are not available, many countries experienced further decline into the mid-1980s; in England, for example, the number of full-time pupils in maintained primary schools fell from 3,970,197 in January 1980 to 3,372,318 in January 1985.

In England perhaps the most obvious changes resulting from falling rolls have been institutional ones in the form of school closures and amalgamations. The number of primary schools has fallen from 20,942 in 1973 to 20,454 in 1980 and

19,068 in 1985. In addition, though exact figures are not available, there have been a very large number of amalgamations usually involving the amalgamation of separate infant and junior schools, but also the combining of separate infant schools or separate junior schools. Such changes have resulted in a sharp decrease in the number of separate infant schools — institutions long established within the English system and often regarded as providing many exemplars of interesting practice in the education of young children. In the management of local education authorities, school size has become a critical factor, not just in terms of the numbers of pupils in very small rural (and urban) schools but in terms of schools having the necessary range and mix of teacher experience and expertise to provide the kind of broad, redefined primary curriculum discussed later in this paper.

Within schools, falling rolls have resulted in an increase in mixed-age classes which have produced considerable pedagogic problems for teachers not accustomed to them. Very significantly, too, reorganization has led to many teachers having to work in institutions covering a wider age range or having to be redeployed to other schools. In consequence, institutional and age-range loyalties have been weakened and teachers' professional identities reshaped. While reorganization has meant enforced mobility for some staff, for others it has reduced opportunities for movement through promotion. Stresses and strains in the form of professional and personal problems of readjustment have severely tested the high quality of interpersonal relationships generally characteristic of English primary education.

During the last 20 years, societies in Western Europe have witnessed considerable changes in the patterns of domestic life which have influenced the upbringing of children, their social and emotional development and, less directly, their ability to cope with the range of demands resulting from attendance at primary school. As the Council of Europe's Steering Committee on Population (1982) reports 'Better education and vocational training, increased opportunities for employment outside the home, the possibility to plan family size effectively and responsibly and the elimination of the fear of unwanted pregnancy have made many more women more independent' than previously. Moves towards greater equality between the sexes have resulted in a blurring of the distinctions between the roles of men and women, both within the home and within the work place. Since 1965 there has been a great increase in the proportion of women in the labour force (currently about 42 per cent in the United Kingdom) and, more recently, with the steep rise in male unemployment, an increase in the number of men at home. In many homes, men and women are sharing responsibilities and tasks to a greater degree than formerly; relationships are becoming more fluid and less predictable as couples negotiate and then renegotiate their roles in the family situation. An increasing number of children live in 'one-parent families' or in a number of different domestic situations as their parents remarry or live with other partners after their divorce. In Britain, the effects of such changing patterns on young children's development and receptivity to the intellectual and interpersonal demands of primary schools have not been documented in research terms.

Changes in domestic patterns are but one aspect of a more pervasive cultural phenomenon which has been recognized in Western Europe — the development of increasingly pluralistic societies where variations in individual and group values, beliefs and lifestyles are acknowledged, though not universally welcomed or encouraged. *Cultural pluralism* of a limited kind is not a new phenomenon, since class and regional variations have long been established, but significant in recent decades are the extent to which established views, expectations and assumptions have been openly and widely challenged and the added pluralistic dimensions to cultural life which have resulted from the settlement of ethnic minority groups from former European colonies. Broadfoot (1985) describes this weakening of the normative consensus underpinning society:

> The cultural 'roots' of education policy — like other areas of social life — are increasingly unstable. Affluence, rising expectations, the media, technical innovation and modern forms of communication, the decline of religion and the success of modern science, have all broken up the traditional life-world of more strictly constrained life choices. As the horizons for self-identity are pushed out to embrace a broadening range of alternative forms of life and a myriad of possible futures, traditions are robbed of their authority. They lose their normative force. The more multi-cultural societies become, the more there is a corresponding weakening of consensus. (p. 276)

The challenge facing primary schools in societies such as England, which are both multi-racial and culturally diverse, is to value and respond to diversity amongst the children and at the same time to foster a sense of social cohesion through the pursuit of common aspirations and values.

Economic factors have been, and seem likely to remain, particularly potent influences on developments within educational systems. In the 1960s, high rates of economic growth, low inflation and political and public confidence in education as a major investment in future economic growth resulted in a general expansion of educational systems in Western Europe, involving, at the primary stage, improvements in teacher–pupil ratios, accommodation, resources and support services for children and teachers. However, the late 1970s and 1980s have been characterized in economic terms by reductions in manufacturing output and a steep rise in unemployment (in the United Kingdom, for example, the percentage of the working population who were unemployed rose from 6.8 per cent in 1980 to 13.5 per cent in 1985). Education systems have shared in the general depression, as many governments in Western Europe stressed greater value for public money and instigated reductions in public expenditure. Parallel with these developments, many states reduced expenditure on primary education as a percentage of total public current expenditure on education; falling pupil enrolments in the primary sector contributed to such governmental savings. In England and Wales, the period of financial constraint at both national and local education authority levels has had its effects, not primarily on staffing ratios which continued to improve until 1984, but on other aspects of primary education. Some of the partial effects, direct or indirect, of financial constraint are documented in HM Inspectorate's expenditure report based on visits to 1,600 maintained primary and secondary schools in the autumn term of

1985: though stressing that 'links between resources and quality are not straight-forward' and pointing out the 'marked need for efficient and effective management of people and resources at every level' and 'for improved leadership', the report identifies a statistically significant association between satisfactory or better levels of appropriate resources and work of sound quality, and between unsatisfactory levels of resources and poor quality work (DES, 1986c, p. 6). It goes on:

> Of the resource factors associated with work judged less than satisfactory in the primary schools visited, the most frequently identified was unsatisfactory or unsuitable accommodation . . . this was followed, in descending order, by the inadequate provision of books, either in number, quality or appropriateness; the lack of sufficient equipment; inappropriate furniture; and poor quality or unsuitable school-produced teaching materials. Of the non-resource factors identified as adversely affecting the quality of work in primary schools, the most commonly referred to was teaching groups containing pupils with a very wide range of ability or of mixed age. Together, these factors were affecting some 1,270 lessons or just over a quarter of the total. (p. 15)

Technological changes, particularly the development of micro-processing and robotics, are influencing the context and, to an increasing though limited extent, the content of the primary curriculum in England and elsewhere in Europe. In recent years, micro-technology has been held responsible for a significant proportion of the growing unemployment in Western Europe; it seems set fair to be a major influence on the incidence of paid employment in the future, on the kinds of competencies required of those in paid employment, and on the patterns of work and leisure, enjoyed, or endured, by the majority of the population. The availability of cheap micro-computers has direct implications for teaching in primary class-rooms and is necessitating an examination of the most fruitful uses to which these powerful tools can be put, and of the kinds of capabilities and attitudes children need to acquire if they are to interact profitably with micro-computers.

English Primary Education and the Primary Curriculum

Against the backcloth of economic, technological, demographic and cultural changes outlined in the previous section, what issues have been developing specifically in English primary education? The first is a highly generalized but very significant development — concerned with changes in the way primary education and the primary curriculum are being thought about and discussed. Until the mid-1970s, discussion about primary education was characterized by a kind of two-party oppositional 'politics' — between adherents of what has variously been termed as the 'developmental', 'progressive' or 'liberal romantic' perspective on the one hand and the 'elementary', 'utilitarian' or 'conservative' perspective on the other. It is possible to characterize the two perspectives briefly and without undue distortion. The 'liberal romantic' view of primary education, exemplified most clearly but not totally in the Plowden Report (CACE, 1967), starts from, and constantly refers back to, the individual child when developing educational principles. It celebrates self-expression, individual autonomy, first-hand experience, discovery learning and personal growth. Compared with other perspectives, it advocates a much more equal partnership of teacher and taught with teachers, to some extent at least, learning 'alongside' children; it emphasizes the processes of learning rather than its products; and it offers children a relatively high degree of choice (though still somewhat circumscribed) in the type, content and duration of activities. The 'elementary' tradition, in contrast, views the curriculum as a repository of essential subject matter and skills which need to be handed down or transmitted by teachers in an orderly, systematic way. It stresses products rather than processes, reception rather than discovery learning, social and intellectual distance rather than partnership between teachers and children. It offers children little or no discretion in the content or style of the learning they undertake.

Since the mid- or late 1970s, a third perspective — 'liberal pragmatism' — has become increasingly prominent in professional discussion of primary education. This holds a middle ground position, viewing the curriculum as a set of learning experiences largely, but not entirely, determined by teachers but respecting to some extent both the individuality of children and the importance of cultural transmission. Advocates of liberal pragmatism advocate a broad curricular grounding for all children, in part preparatory for secondary education, but a grounding which takes account of the fact that children learn through both first-hand and second-hand experiences, which uses children's knowledge and interests as starting points and contributions to on-going work but which shapes and refines children's experience along teacher-structured lines. The approach seeks to be both liberal, in giving a broad range of experience through a variety of teaching and learning styles, and pragmatic, in building on and extending much current practice. It is characterized, too, by a concern for planning and policy-making at school and local authority levels, for systematic progression and continuity between and within schools, and for evaluation and assessment of children's learning at each level from the class to the education system nationally. The last 10 years have witnessed the gradual formulation, refinement and public expression of this view of primary education; the perspective has set, and continues to set, the agenda for discussion and policy-making in English primary education.[1]

As a result of the influence of liberal pragmatism and its concerns for planning and policy-making, the primary curriculum is coming under increasing scrutiny — not just the teaching and learning activities offered within it, but the very way it is conceptualized. Despite this development, the long-established subject-based framework for the curriculum is alive and well and living in the minds and, to some extent, the practices of many policy-makers and teachers, the result in part of their own primary and secondary education. Its attraction is very strong, as witnessed by the fact that even the Plowden Report (CACE, 1967), while acknowledging that children's learning did not fall into neat subject compartments, went on to discuss the curriculum very largely under separate subject headings. To some teachers, subjects appear to be almost 'natural components of any curriculum'; to others, who acknowledge their 'artificial' and social construction, they are extremely convenient categories for curriculum analysis and review; to others they are an irrelevance and a reactionary irrelevance at that. The newer frameworks for discussing the primary curriculum, discussed in this section, are attempts to define, and trace interrelationships among, the constituent elements of a primary curriculum to which all children should be introduced — elements drawing on, but going beyond, established subjects.

HM Inspectorate's report of the national primary survey (DES, 1978) is one such attempt. It distinguishes skills and attitudes recurring in various parts of the curriculum and analyses the work of primary children under five headings: a) language and literacy; b) mathematics; c) science (experimental and observational); d) social studies; and e) aesthetic and physical education. As judged by the recently published findings of a DES survey (DES, 1986d), this framework has become an established part of the curricular policies adopted by a number of local education authorities. In an essay published in 1984, Blyth offers a six-fold categorization — 'not subjects or, necessarily, forms of understanding or endeavour, but rather six elements in children's lives' (p. 53) — which need to be incorporated into what he terms an 'enabling curriculum': a) growth, health and movement; b) communication (through a variety of codes — linguistic, numerical, graphical, electronic, physical); c) interpretation of the social and physical world; d) vision and imagination; e) feeling, expression and appreciation, especially through the arts; f) values and attitudes.

Recently, HM Inspectorate have put forward, as a basis for discussion, a six-fold framework for the analysis, review and development of the curriculum — primary as well as secondary (DES, 1985e). This comprises: i) general aims; ii) areas of learning and experience; iii) elements of learning; iv) cross-curricular issues; v) general characteristics of the curriculum; vi) assessment. The discussion document has met with general approval from local education authorities and from national professional associations; its discussion in many schools has unfortunately been hindered by industrial action; its reception by tutors in institutions of higher education has been mixed, some commending its basis in cultural analysis and the usefulness of its framework as an analytic tool, others critical of some of its distinctions as epistemologically suspect.

Whether through the primary survey's five broad categories, Blyth's six elements, or HM Inspectorate's nine areas, primary schools are being challenged to consider the structure of the whole curriculum and to do what some have done already, i.e. readjusting emphases, widening curricular opportunities. In this way they will move away from what Alexander (1983) terms 'the two curricula syndrome' whereby mathematics and English are given far greater importance, far greater time allocation, many more resources, more systematic planning and more considered evaluation and assessment than other parts of the curriculum. Acceptance of the view that, for example, all nine areas of learning and experience are essential to children's education leads at the very least to schools reviewing the human, temporal and material resources devoted to constituent parts of the curriculum to see whether there are any unjustifiable imbalances which need to be redressed. Issues such as priority, range and balance within the curriculum are now having to be addressed systematically and explicitly. Their consideration inevitably involves the making of practical judgments concerning the extent to which aspirations are currently being realized, and the exercising of value judgments regarding desirable re-emphases or alterations to existing practice. The uncertain nature of both these kinds of professional judgment does not obviate the necessity of making them nor of involving all teaching staff and governors (and perhaps also non-teaching staff), as the ILEA Report (1985) suggests in the discussion and resolution of such issues.

Such a review is made even more necessary by the ever-broadening range of curricular demands being made on schools. Aspects of health education (e.g. DES, 1986b), environmental education, political education (e.g. Harwood, 1985, 1986), education for family life (e.g. DES, 1985c), world studies (e.g. Fisher and Hicks, 1985), technology (e.g. Williams, 1985; Williams and Jinks, 1985), information technology (e.g. Wagstaffe, 1988) and industry education (e.g. Jamieson et al., 1984), to name but a few, are pressing their claims as offering worthwhile, particularly relevant experiences to children at an age where their attitudes are being formed and basic views of the physical and social world are established. Equally, the increasing recognition of discrimination on the basis of gender and/or race — leading in some local education authorities and schools to explicit policies to counter racism and sexism — is also placing demands on teachers to reappraise teaching methods, forms of organization and programmes of work in all curricular areas. The 'over-loading' of the primary curriculum can only be prevented if schools reject an 'additive' model of curriculum design (whereby new areas are simply tacked on to existing work) and instead adopt a thorough-going review, perhaps taking several years, of their programmes of work using criteria such as those proposed by HM Inspectorate (1985) to see which established elements need to be retained, which de-emphasized, which perhaps omitted entirely and which new elements ought to be incorporated, not necessarily as discrete entities but perhaps as facets or dimensions to existing areas of work. In relation to the problem of overload, it is important to stress, and hopefully it is comforting for primary schools to acknowledge, that 'a single activity can contribute to several areas of learning. When learning to cook, for example, 6-year-olds can extend their vocabulary and oral skills; learn to recognize simple mathematical relationships; be trained in hygiene; and improve their manual dexterity' (DES, 1985e, para. 34).

As yet a further dimension to this re-examination of the curriculum, the nature of the 'basic skills' developed in primary schools is being redefined to include a range of higher level capabilities previously considered by some schools to be applicable for only a minority of children. *The Curriculum from 5 to 16* (DES, 1985e, para. 100) offers a tentative classification of such redefined 'basics' which need to be practised and refined by all children during their time in primary school. The national primary survey (DES, 1978) helped set this trend in train; successive middle school surveys (DES, 1983, 1985b) have continued it. It is being argued that individually, in small groups, or through whole class discussion, primary children of all ages need to be given more opportunities to pose questions, to offer explanations, to predict and to speculate. They need greater encouragement to test their ideas through conducting experiments, designing structures, inventing artefacts or undertaking enquiries; through selecting and evaluating evidence; and through establishing tentative conclusions, patterns or generalizations. Such higher-level capabilities based, for their proper application, on understanding related to particular areas of learning and experience are regarded as the heart of successful primary practice. They are not easy to foster in the crowded ecological setting of the primary classroom, as HM Inspectorate's surveys and other research studies indicate, but are characteristic of teaching and learning in some schools.

The development of a wide range of approaches is a challenge not only to practitioners, but also to researchers who have examined teaching and learning in primary classrooms over the last decade, but who, according to Simon (1985), have not yet developed adequate pedagogic theories to account for or to guide practice. Nowhere is this lack more evident than in relation to the related issues of match (DES, 1978; Bennett et al., 1984) and differentiation, i.e. providing children with learning experiences which take due account of their differing characteristics and yet which are guided by a common set of principles and purposes which transcend these differences. In his paper, which links the neglect of pedagogy in England with the issue of differentiation, Simon (1985) argues that:

> To develop effective pedagogic means involves starting ... from what children have in common as members of the human species; to establish the general principles of teaching and, in the light of this, to determine what modifications of practice are necessary to meet specific individual needs. If all children are to be assisted to learn, to master increasingly complex cognitive tasks, to develop increasingly complex skills and abilities or mental operations, then this is an objective that schools must have in common; their task becomes the deliberate development of such skills and abilities in all their children. And this involves importing a definite structure into the teaching, and so into the learning experiences provided for the pupils. Individual differences only become important, in this context, if the pedagogic means elaborated are found not to be appropriate to particular children (or groups of children) because of one or other aspect of their individual development or character. In this situation, the requirement becomes that of modifying the pedagogical means so that they become appropriate for all; that is, of applying general principles in specific instances. (p. 99)

If progress is to be made on the elucidation of general principles of teaching and learning and on appropriate forms of differentiation, researchers have not only to focus more on learning and on the curriculum in the classroom context but also to involve teachers much more as collaborators and 'critical friends' in the research enterprise. More than this, more teachers need to be encouraged to take a research stance towards their practice: systematically enquiring into it and its effects, and making their findings known to fellow practitioners inside and outside the research community. Despite the claims made by some of its proponents, this 'teacher as researcher' movement, a development of the 1970s, is a frail plant requiring careful nurturing in the bracing climate of the 1980s if it is to make a major contribution to understanding classroom practice and developing the professionality of teachers.

As outlined in paragraph 81 of *Better Schools* (DES, 1985a), another current development is the attempt to define more closely the kinds of skills and understandings children should be able to exhibit, bearing in mind the diversity of abilities and rates of development amongst 11-year-olds. The difficulty of this exercise is readily acknowledged: 'It will be no short or easy task to move towards a more precise definition of attainment targets' (para. 81). The aim is to establish at national level sets of reasonable expectations in different curricular areas, which 'at school level . . . can and should be finely tuned to accommodate particular classes and indeed pupils' (DES, 1986a, para. 24). Papers in the HMI series *Curriculum Matters*, findings from the Assessment of Performance Unit (APU), accounts of 'good practice' by HM Inspectorate and specially commissioned research in the area of primary mathematics are all helping to clarify expectations. This work is being paralleled in local authorities such as Croydon where expectations of performance at primary level have been made explicit (Croydon, 1985). The effort at a more precise definition is based on the belief that this will help all concerned to assess the effectiveness of policies and practice at national, local and school levels; will encourage teachers to have appropriately high expectations of children; and will help motivate the pupils. It needs to be stressed that the aim is not to produce a highly specific set of minimum attainment targets to be reached by all pupils — a 1980s equivalent of the Revised Code of the last century.

Two other major curricular issues, continuity and consistency, could feature specifically in an overview such as this but can, for convenience, be subsumed in a last overall issue — the emergence of the curriculum as an object of policy at national, local, and, increasingly, school levels. Nationally, central government has an explicit policy, i.e. to secure 'a broad agreement about the objectives and content of the school curriculum' and is pursuing this through seeking consensus in four areas: the purposes of learning at school; the contribution of each main subject area or element to the curriculum as a whole; the organization and content of the 5–16 curriculum; and statements of expectations of pupils' performance, as discussed in the previous paragraph. A number of general aims have been agreed (DES, 1985a, para. 44); a number of fundamental principles enunciated (breadth, balance, relevance and differentiation); a discussion paper on the organization and content of the 5–16 curriculum issued (DES, 1984b); and other work undertaken including the publication of the *Curriculum Matters* series. In the area of science, a definitive policy statement has been issued (DES, 1985d) setting out an overall approach, highlighting priorities and, at the primary level, listing broad criteria for the selection of content, as well as areas of study in which children's understanding of scientific concepts should be developed and factors important in the successful implementation of primary science. Through these initiatives it is hoped to achieve a measure of continuity and consistency nationally such that all pupils 'have access to a curriculum of similar breadth and balance irrespective of their level of ability, the school they attend or their social circumstances' (DES, 1985e, para. 3).

With the passing of the 1986 Education Act, local education authorities are also being required to have curricular policies to inform the execution of their duties, especially in relation to such matters as staff development, the deployment of the teaching force and the advisory service, and the achievement of a continuous 5–16 curriculum. Judging from a recently published report (DES, 1986c), at least five-sixths of authorities have already drawn up curriculum policy statements or plan to do so, some covering the 5–16 curriculum as a whole and some dealing separately with primary and secondary curricula. Finally, schools are being urged to formulate policy statements embodying their general educational intentions and establishing appropriate expectations relating to the wide range of their children's abilities, aptitudes and educational needs (DES, 1983, 1985b). Such an approach to curricular policy-making demands conscious and coordinated planning by primary practitioners; it does not deny the importance of individual teacher flair or opportunism but assumes that these are not sufficient to secure children's entitlement to a broad, balanced and relevant primary education. Concerted action by primary staff, along the lines discussed in the next section, is being recommended.

Staff Development and Deployment

The curricular trends discussed in the previous section are necessitating the re-examination and the reinterpretation of the task of primary teachers in relation both to their 'own' classes and to their colleagues. Several major findings from the national primary survey (DES, 1978) have provided the foundation from which this reappraisal has developed: i) the effectiveness of a broad curriculum involving the application of basic skills to other areas (para. 8.29); ii) the lack of sufficiently consistent coverage for important aspects of the curriculum, thereby putting a broad curriculum 'at risk' in some schools (para. 6.09); iii) the beneficial influence of some post-holders on the quality of work (paras 4.5 and 7.36).

In many schools, ways are now being sought of tapping the curricular and pedagogic expertise of individual members of staff (not just post-holders) for the benefit of the school as a whole in order to develop and keep under review a redefined curriculum which provides consistent coverage of important areas and elements and which encourages the development and application of higher-level 'basic' skills. Such attempts are based on the beliefs that it is no longer reasonable to expect class teachers to cope individually and unaided with the range of demands now being made on them, and that individual self-sufficiency is undesirable in any case in view of the importance of continuity of experience and reasonable consistency of approach from class to class within the same school. In the light of such beliefs, four aspects of the primary teacher's role are undergoing re-examination: curriculum coordination, class teaching, collaboration with parents, and involvement in school-wide review and policy-making. Progress in this reinterpretation varies from school to school and from aspect to aspect.

Since the publication of the primary survey, many local education authorities and heads, with the encouragement of the DES and HM Inspectorate, have made considerable efforts to develop the role of curriculum coordinators or consultants in primary schools. Increasingly, not just post-holders are involved; there is often an expectation that all, or almost all, members of staff, including relatively inexperienced teachers, will take on a coordinating role for an aspect of the curriculum. Job descriptions for coordinators are commonplace and, in some cases, arrangements are in hand for reviewing progress in relation to the discharge of responsibilities so described. In some, though not all, schools such coordinators are now regarded as central to curricular review and development: formulating and monitoring programmes of work, giving advice, managing resources, keeping in touch with developments in their curricular area, providing advice on the school's needs for inservice education, and, less often, running school-based inservice sessions, offering exemplars of classroom practice which colleagues can observe and discuss, and working alongside teachers in the class situation. Fulfilling a coordinating role requires a range of demanding skills (Campbell, 1985) as well as sensitive support from headteachers, access to outside advice, ideas and facilities, and, most particularly, time during the school day to observe the work being done and to guide and support other teachers in the class context. Headteachers have a key role to play in helping establish the legitimacy and value of the coordinator's role, particularly through encouraging and persuading class teachers to welcome advice from their peers as an accepted part of normal, professional practice. Developing coordinators' subject-matter expertise and their knowledge of how children might engage with that subject matter is also very important, if the programmes of work they devise and the advice they offer are to be soundly based. Developments in initial teacher training, involving students studying a subject or area of the primary curriculum for two years at a level appropriate to higher education, are intended to develop this expertise and confidence among new entrants to the primary teaching profession (DES, 1984a).

Although some progress has been made in clarifying the nature of the coordinating or consultancy role and in enhancing its standing, there is far less clarity, and more apprehension, among teachers generally concerning the implications of recent curricular thinking about the place of the class teacher. Some have foreseen the dismantling, or at the very least, the weakening, of the class-teacher system, particularly in the upper part of primary schools. It needs to be stressed that the long-standing and valued tradition that one teacher should be responsible for ensuring that his/her class receives a curriculum adequate in range and depth is not seriously 'at risk', but the way this responsibility is to be properly exercised and supported is being reinterpreted in the light of the changes and developments outlined earlier. It is being argued that the class-teacher system needs strengthening through sensitive deployment and development of the expertise which already exists on primary school staffs by means of a variety of ploys, varying from the one-off occasion, through temporary short-term arrangements, to more permanent long-term procedures, all subject to modification as circumstances change. Support for the class teacher could take one or more of a variety of forms, depending on the individual and the area of the curriculum in question: occasional advice from a coordinator or other member of staff with specialist knowledge; a detailed scheme of work identifying concepts, skills, subject matter and attitudes to be developed and giving guidance on organization, methodology, differentiation and assessment; attendance at inservice courses run by outside agencies or by school personnel; cooperative teaching with one or more colleagues; help for a period from an advisory teacher; a coordinator working alongside a colleague for a time to help introduce a new aspect of work; or, in some cases, perhaps most often (but not necessarily only) with older children, a member of staff with specialist knowledge teaching someone else's class a particular aspect of the curriculum for a month, a term or a year, provided the class teacher retains overall responsibility for the work of the class, including the links that would need to be made between his/her own work and that of the specialist. Ideally, as a class teacher, an individual member of staff would have access to support such as this in each area of the curriculum except the one for which he or she had coordinating responsibility; in that area he/she would be expected to provide support to colleagues.

The fostering of collaborative rather than individualistic modes of working is also illustrated by moves involving the renegotiation of home–school relationships so that parents are not only informed about, but also actively involved in, their children's *school* education in a way which complements the more general educative influence they can exert through the many experiences of family life, including the fostering of particular interests and hobbies. This renegotiation is particularly manifest in those schools which are collaborating with parents so that children's learning in class is deliberately reinforced and enriched by experiences at home jointly planned, at least in part, by teachers and parents. The most obvious sign of this partnership in children's home learning is the proliferation of schemes involving parents systematically in their children's reading following the startlingly positive effects of such practices, particularly in socially disadvantaged areas, noted in research, for example, by Hewison and Tizard (1980), Tizard, Schofield and Hewison (1981) and by Widlake and Macleod (1984). Similar parental involvement schemes are now being launched for mathematics. Of course, parental involvement in children's school learning through provision of experiences at home has long occurred on an ad hoc basis; the harnessing and coordination of such activities are increasingly being seen as an extremely valuable supplement to schools' efforts. To be optimally effective, such coordination needs the long-term commitment of the whole staff and is thus a policy matter for schools; it also requires the development of a subtly different range of skills as teachers take on the role, however limited, of adult educationist, albeit with a primary education focus. Such collaboration also has far-reaching implications for the kinds of learning activities provided in school time and to which parental activities are to be related: for example, more of the same at home might well be unproductive in the long term, despite its short-term reinforcing effects. Home–school cooperation in relation to the teaching of reading and, increasingly mathematics, is a particularly topical exemplar of a more general phenomenon — the increasing involvement of parents in the work of the education service, not just in England but in Western Europe more generally.

Perhaps the most difficult to realize of the four role adjustments called for by recent developments relates to the development of what Campbell (1985) terms 'collegiality' — participatory decision-taking by the staff as a whole. Primary teachers have traditionally seen themselves as relatively autonomous in their classrooms but having little influence on the school as a whole (Taylor et al., 1972): they are teachers first and members of the school's staff second. They are now being asked to take a collaborative rather than individualistic approach to their work — not just in relation to curriculum planning and review but in terms of decisions relating to issues such as the identification of the school's INSET needs under the new INSET grant arrangements, links with parents and the wider community, and liaison with other schools and outside agencies. This 'collegial' approach may be manifest in the formulation and endorsement of policies for particular areas of the curriculum or in relation to issues such as anti-racism or anti-sexism; it may take the form of school self-evaluation activities using local education authority materials or schemes such as Guidelines for Internal Review and Development in Schools (GRIDS) (MacMahon et al., 1984) to tackle issues springing directly from the felt concerns of staff; it may lead to the production of school development plans such as those advocated in the ILEA report on primary schools (ILEA, 1985). The development of collegiality has implications for the inservice education of teachers who will need greater understanding of interpersonal and group processes to participate effectively; it also has implications for the role of heads whose basis of authority may increasingly rest, not on their formal position, but on their skills in facilitating colleagues' participation and in helping them solve problems and resolve conflicts (Coulson, 1988). In some areas, the concept of collegiality is being extended to other schools in the locality, as groups of schools meet to develop and coordinate their work and to engage jointly in inservice education. As Campbell points out, the collegial school may still be more of an image than a reality, though a significant number of schools are developing along these lines.

Conclusion

The issues raised in this paper bear witness to the fact that during the last decade, despite MacLure's 'disciplines of contraction', policy and practice in English primary education have continued to develop — in response both to outside forces and to the education system's own dynamic. The issues highlighted are not the only ones affecting, or likely to affect, primary schools; for example, changes in the initial training of teachers or issues related to equal opportunities are not discussed here in detail but are likely to prove influential in many schools. The task of the primary teacher has never been easy, either for novitiates aware of their shortcomings or for experienced practitioners aware of the inevitable gap between professional aspiration and achievement. Recent developments and issues have served to make that task even more demanding but have, helpfully, highlighted the impossibility of individual self-sufficiency in discharging it. They make it more necessary than ever for those involved in primary education, individually and collectively, to clarify aspirations, to learn from the experience of their pursuit, and so to redefine issues, modify practice and renew those aspirations. It is, however, important to set high expectations for professional development as well as for the development of pupils, despite the inevitability of a degree of disappointment when these are not fully met. As Stenhouse pointed out, 'Success can be achieved only by lowering our sights. The future is more powerfully formed by our commitment to those enterprises we think it worth pursuing, even though we fall short of our aspirations ... we shall only teach better if we learn intelligently from the experience of shortfall, both in our grasp of the knowledge we offer and of our knowledge of how to offer it' (quoted in Rudduck and Hopkins, 1985, pp. 125–6).

Note

1 Alternative perspectives on changing modes of thought related to primary education are provided by Golby (1982) and Blyth (1984).

References

ALEXANDER, R. (1983) 'Training for primary class teaching: An agenda for progress', *Primary Education Review*, 16.

BENNETT, N., DESFORGES, C., COCKBURN, A. and WILKINSON, B. (1984) *The Quality of Pupil Learning Experiences*, Hove, Lawrence Erlbaum Associates.

BLYTH, W. (1984) *Development, Experience and Curriculum in Primary Education*, London: Croom Helm.

BROADFOOT, P. (1985) 'Changing patterns of educational accountability in England and France', *Comparative Education*, **21**, 3.

CAMPBELL, R. (1985) *Developing the Primary School Curriculum*, London: Holt Rinehart and Winston.

CENTRAL ADVISORY COUNCIL FOR EDUCATION (ENGLAND) (CACE) (1967) *Children and Their Primary Schools* (The Plowden Report), London: HMSO.

COULSON, A. (1988) 'An approach to headship development through personal and professional growth', in CLARKSON, M. (ed.) *Emerging Issues in Primary Education*, London: Falmer Press.

CROYDON (1985) *Primary Education in Croydon*, London: Croydon.

DEPARTMENT OF EDUCATION AND SCIENCE (1978) *Primary Education in England*, London: HMSO.

DEPARTMENT OF EDUCATION AND SCIENCE (1983) *9–13 Middle Schools*, London: HMSO.

DEPARTMENT OF EDUCATION AND SCIENCE (1984a) *Initial Teacher Training: Approval of Courses* (Circular 3/84), London: HMSO.

DEPARTMENT OF EDUCATION AND SCIENCE (1984b) *The Organization and Content of the 5–16 Curriculum*, London: HMSO.

DEPARTMENT OF EDUCATION AND SCIENCE (1985a) *Better Schools* (Cmnd 9469), London: HMSO.

DEPARTMENT OF EDUCATION AND SCIENCE (1985b) *Education 8–12 in Combined and Middle Schools*, London: HMSO.

DEPARTMENT OF EDUCATION AND SCIENCE (1985c) *Home Economics from 5–16*, Curriculum Matters Series 5, London: HMSO.

DEPARTMENT OF EDUCATION AND SCIENCE (1985d) *Science 5–16*, London: HMSO.

DEPARTMENT OF EDUCATION AND SCIENCE (1985e) *The Curriculum from 5–16*, Curriculum Matters Series 2, London: HMSO.

DEPARTMENT OF EDUCATION AND SCIENCE (1986a) *English from 5–16: The Responses to Curriculum Matters Series I*, London: HMSO.

DEPARTMENT OF EDUCATION AND SCIENCE (1986b) *Health Education from 5–16*, Curriculum Matters Series 6, London: HMSO.

DEPARTMENT OF EDUCATION AND SCIENCE (1986c) *Local Authority Policies for the School Curriculum*, London: HMSO.

DEPARTMENT OF EDUCATION AND SCIENCE (1986d) *Report by HM Inspectors on the Effects of Local Authority Expenditure Policies on Educational Provision in England, 1985*, London: HMSO.

FISHER, S. and HICKS, D. (1985) *World Studies 8–13 — A Teacher's Handbook*, London: Oliver and Boyd.

GOLBY, M. (1982) 'Micro-computers and the primary curriculum', in GARLAND, R. (ed.) *Microcomputers and Children in the Primary School*, London: Falmer Press.

HARWOOD, D. (1985) 'We need political not Political Education for 5–13 year olds', *Education 3–13*, **13**, 1.

HARWOOD, D. (1986) 'To advocate or to educate?', *Education 3–13*, **14**, 1.

HEWISON, J. and TIZARD, J. (1980) 'Parental involvement and reading attainment', *British Journal of Educational Psychology*, 50.

ILEA (1985) *Improving Primary Schools*, London: ILEA.

JAMIESON, I. (1984) *We Make Kettles: Studying Industry in the Primary School*, Harlow: Longman.

MACLURE, S. (1984) *Educational Development and School Building: Aspects of Public Policy 1945–1973*, Harlow: Longman.

MACMAHON, A., BOLAM, R., HOLLY, P. and ABBOTT, R. (1984) *Guidelines for Internal Review and Development in Schools: Primary School Handbook*, Harlow: Longman.

RUDDUCK, J. and HOPKINS, D. (eds) (1985) *Research as a Basis for Teaching: Readings from the Work of Lawrence Stenhouse*, London: Heinemann.

SIMON, B. (1985) *Does Education Matter?*, London: Lawrence and Wishart.

STEERING COMMITEE ON POPULATION (1982) *Conclusions* (Conference Report), European Population Conference, Council of Europe, Strasbourg.

TAYLOR, P., REID, W., HOLLEY, B. and EXON, G. (1972) *Purpose, Power and Constraint in the Primary School Curriculum*, Basingstoke: Macmillan.

TIZARD, J., SCHOFIELD, W. and HEWISON, J. (1981) 'Collaboration between teachers and parents in assisting children's reading', *British Journal of Educational Psychology*, 52.

WAGSTAFFE, A. (1988) 'Emerging issues in micro-computing', in CLARKSON, M. (ed.) *Emerging Issues in Primary Education*, London, Falmer Press.

WIDLAKE, P. and MACLEOD, F. (1984) *Raising Standards: Parental Involvement Programmes and the Language Performance of Children*, Coventry: Community Education Development Centre.

WILLIAMS, P. (1985) *Teaching Craft, Design and Technology Five to Thirteen*, London: Croom Helm.

WILLIAMS, P. and JINKS, D. (1985) *Design and Technology 5–12*, London: Falmer Press.

6 Primary Education: Issues in the Early 1990s

Whereas inspection by OFSTED dominated the professional (and in some cases personal) lives of primary school teachers between 1994 and 1998, the predominant concern in the first half of the 1990s was having to come to terms with the curriculum and assessment requirements brought about by the Education Reform Act (ERA) of 1988. Though, in retrospect, the introduction of a national curriculum seemed inevitable given the developments of the previous decade, the need to teach a legally mandated curriculum for the first time this century proved both challenging and threatening to the primary teaching profession in the years following 1988. In the event the challenge was met — very successfully in some cases, reasonably effectively in most. Many schools were able to successfully 'domesticate' its requirements (scaled down following the Dearing Review of 1993), though usually after very considerable struggle, overload and heart-searching. The same was true but to a lesser extent of assessment and testing, though anxiety about their uses and effects has remained long after the frustration and anger caused by annual changes in assessment policy have been exhausted.

In the early days of the National Curriculum, the 'what' of primary education took precedence over the 'how'. However, from 1991 onwards, central government and its agencies took an increasing interest in issues of internal school organization and pedagogy and attempted to influence professional opinion through ministerial pronouncements, discussion papers and conferences but not through legislation (see Chapter 13). Pedagogy proved more resistant to change than curriculum or assessment, but change it did . . . slowly. Probably the most successful, and widely appreciated, of the ERA initiatives was local management of schools, which gave schools much more control over their own finances and helped them develop a less dependent relationship with their LEAs. However, this success was bought at a cost in some schools where managerialism rather than educational leadership was the order of the day. This chapter, written in 1994, captures some of the dominant issues of the early 1990s.

Introduction

Primary education is the subject of much political and professional interest. The government has identified primary education as a major focus in its concern to improve standards. Political interest in issues of teaching methods, groupings and curriculum organization, instigated by a former Secretary of State, Kenneth Clarke, has been sustained by his successors. There are professional challenges, too, coming in part from the Office for Standards in Education (OFSTED), which are asking, not yet requiring, primary teachers to review and, where necessary, modify their teaching techniques, forms of grouping and the ways they organize time and content. More recently the Dearing Review (SCAA, 1993) and the curriculum proposals of the School Curriculum and Assessment Authority (SCAA) have raised major issues related to the planning, teaching and assessment of the National Curriculum, especially in primary schools. The environment surrounding primary schools is changing; primary schools are having to respond.

For convenience the issues facing primary schools are analysed separately under *curriculum, assessment, pedagogy, management* and *funding*, though in practice issues are interrelated in complex ways.

Curriculum

The key factor influencing recent developments in primary education is the phased introduction of the National Curriculum — introduced in 1989 in three subjects in Year 1 and involving by 1993 all nine subjects in Years 1 and 4 and a varying number of subjects in Years 2, 3, 5 and 6. Managing the phased introduction of the National Curriculum has been, and continues to be, a major preoccupation of most primary schools. Preparing for and managing the revised, scaled-down National Curriculum from Autumn 1995 onwards will increasingly be a preoccupation.

Schools have to address the issue of *breadth* — providing all nine core and other foundation subjects and religious education to children in all classes; teaching the full range of attainment targets and related programmes of study; considering whether and how to make provision for the teaching of cross-curricular issues; and deciding what subjects or aspects, if any (for example, a modern foreign language) should be added to the National Curriculum to complete children's curricular entitlement.

A related concept is that of *balance*. Decisions are needed on the balance to be struck between the 'basics' (as defined by Dearing) and the remainder of the curriculum; between the core subjects (especially mathematics and English) and the remaining foundation subjects; between attainment targets within any one subject; and between the National Curriculum and other subjects and aspects. Schools need to decide whether balance ought properly to vary according to key stages or year groups and how it might be 'cashed out' in terms of reasonable time allocations.

A third related issue is that of *coherence*. The curriculum needs to be reasonably coherent both to the teachers planning and teaching it and to the children experiencing it. Relationships and interconnections between subjects and aspects need identifying and capitalizing upon; skills and ideas taught in one area of study need to be applied in others. A form of curriculum organization commonly adopted to foster a measure of coherence (as well as to promote economy in planning and to enhance children's motivation) is *topic work*. The place of separate *subject work* and topic work within the primary curriculum is a key issue. Rarely is it a case of either/or. In most primary schools some subjects have always been taught separately and others, wholly or partly, as aspects of topics. Schools need to decide between different forms of topic work (for example subject-focused or broad-based topics) and between different time frames in which separate subject teaching can be provided. They also need to determine which aspects of the National Curriculum are most appropriately taught through topics and which through separate subjects. Such decisions may properly vary according to factors such as the age of the pupils, the experience and expertise of the teachers and the policies of the schools.

The preparation, implementation and ongoing review of documentation to support the introduction of the revised National Curriculum raise other issues. Primary schools require policy statements to provide general guiding principles for planning, teaching, learning and assessment; schemes of work to give detailed guidance as to how National Curriculum requirements can be met; and, where topic work is employed, arrangements such as whole school or key stage planning frameworks to ensure adequate coverage of statutory requirements, to promote more effective continuity and progression and to avoid undue repetition.

Two interrelated issues dominate current discussion about the primary curriculum. The first relates to the *manageability* of the requirements placed on generalist class teachers — an issue highlighted by the Dearing Review, particularly, but not only, in Key Stage 2. Currently such teachers have to: a) tackle nine subjects and religious education; b) decide whether to give some attention to cross-curricular themes such as health education and environmental education; c) assess, record and report on children's performance; d) respond appropriately to children with special educational needs; and e) plan, prepare and evaluate work to meet a complex span of needs in mixed-ability, and often mixed-age, classes. Related to these demands is the tension between achieving breadth and balance in the curriculum and teaching that curriculum in sufficient depth to match the range of pupils' capabilities. The problem of reconciling depth and breadth of coverage is at the heart of the manageability issue and the future development of the National Curriculum.

Assessment

As a complement to the National Curriculum, assessment requirements have been progressively introduced (and regularly amended on a yearly basis) since 1989. The *testing* has raised questions about the reliability and validity of the tests themselves and the uses to be made of the test data. Early concerns over the practicalities of administration have largely, though not entirely, been replaced by anxieties over the usefulness and, in particular, the uses to be made of the assessment data both within schools and beyond them to draw up 'league tables' in relation to pupils' performance at age 11. The quality of the tests, especially those not yet 'bedded down' at Key Stage 2, also remains an important issue.

Teacher assessment generates anxieties over the lack of research, development and inservice training in this area; over the problems of interpretation deriving from the use of the 8/10-level scale and its statements of attainment and level descriptors;

over the practicalities of administering assessment procedures in over-crowded classrooms; over the validity and reliability of the assessments; and over the extent to which assessment informs planning and teaching.

The *recording* of teacher assessment poses a number of problems for schools and LEAs to resolve. These include the nature of the recording; the degree of detail required by the class teacher herself and by colleagues to whom the children will transfer; the frequency of recording; and the volume of evidence in terms of annotated samples of children's work required to validate teachers' judgments.

Pedagogy

Following the publication of *Curriculum Organisation and Classroom Practice in Primary Schools* (Alexander at al., 1992), primary schools have been asked to consider the strengths and weaknesses of the *teaching techniques* and *organizational* strategies they employ to see if they are 'fit' or 'unfit' for purpose in terms of furthering teachers' learning intentions. An important consideration is the extent to which teachers should engage in direct teaching techniques involving, for example, explaining, questioning and instructing. The balance to be struck between class, group and individual work is another important matter. Teachers need to make conscious decisions about grouping in the light of an appraisal of their potential benefits and drawbacks, rather than as a result of unexamined past practice or adherence to a 'politically correct' orthodoxy. In particular, there is a need to reconsider forms of classroom organization to ensure that teaching time is used to optimum effect and that too many activities are not taking place simultaneously, so diluting the teacher's efforts. A related consideration is how to achieve an acceptable (yet manageable) degree of *differentiation* so that there is a better match of work to the range of children's capabilities. This again involves teachers in reconsidering organizational strategies including the incidence of ability grouping within the class or, where schools are large enough, the introduction of setting across classes.

Management

Management issues revolve around the *leadership role* of the headteacher and the *deployment of staff*. The introduction of the Local Management of Schools has forced primary headteachers (and their governing bodies) to consider carefully the relative importance of the leadership and administrative aspects of their roles. With the help of governing bodies, headteachers need to plan and administer their budgets; they need to be financially accountable; they need to link financial decisions to priorities established in school development plans. But the quality of the school, especially of curriculum leadership, remains a central criterion of their effectiveness (OFSTED, 1994).

Aspects of the leadership role include establishing and articulating a sense of purpose and ethos; coordinating school development planning and policy-making;

monitoring and evaluating the quality of curriculum, teaching and learning; managing staff time, including non-contact time where it can be provided; and being ultimately responsible for staff appraisal and development. Providing a genuine management role for other members of staff, including curriculum coordinators, is an important but subsidiary issue. They, too, need to be able to play a part in developing, implementing and monitoring policies and schemes of work. Creating opportunities for them to do this, especially during the school day, is another test of leadership and management.

A second major management issue relates to the deployment of staff. Primary schools need to consider how the subject and pedagogic expertise of their teachers can best be deployed to provide the children with their curricular entitlement. This might involve complementing the generalist class teacher role with a measure of specialist or semi-specialist teaching in particular year groups or key stages. The deployment of teachers as generalists, semi-specialists or specialists and their professional development are closely interrelated issues.

There are other management issues of importance, all contributing to a formidable range of responsibilities for headteachers: the appraisal of teaching and associate staff; the increasing involvement of primary schools in initial teacher education; the OFSTED inspection of schools, including preparations for, and follow up to, inspections; and the enhanced role of governing bodies in formulating policies, taking financial decisions and devising and implementing post-inspection action plans.

Funding

A fundamental underlying issue is the *differential funding* of primary and secondary schooling. Many, though not all, of the management and curricular issues facing primary schools have resource implications. The readjustment of funding formulae in favour of primary schools, particularly in respect of pupils in Years 5 and 6, is seen as a precondition for resolving many of the issues raised in this paper.

References

ALEXANDER, R., ROSE, J. and WOODHEAD, C. (1992) *Curriculum Organisation and Class-room Practice in Primary Schools*, London: Department of Education and Science.
OFFICE FOR STANDARDS IN EDUCATION (OFSTED) (1994) *Primary Matters*, London: Office for Standards in Education.
SCHOOL CURRICULUM AND ASSESSMENT AUTHORITY (SCAA) (1993) *The National Curriculum and Its Assessment: The Final Report*, London: School Curriculum and Assessment Authority.

Part 2

The Primary Curriculum

7 Changes to the English Primary Curriculum 1862–1988

Neither policy-makers nor educationists have long memories, but both could benefit from the hindsight a knowledge of the recent and more distant past can bring. As has been said previously, primary education is particularly susceptible to myth-making but some knowledge of the past is indispensable in 'debunking' such myths, as well as valuable in informing decisions about future directions and policies. For example, particularly recently but periodically throughout the last century, it has been claimed that primary education has neglected the so-called 'basics'. Such a myth can be easily refuted by those willing to investigate past policy and practice and those willing to hear and reflect on the results of such investigations; literacy and numeracy have long, and always, been seen as the core of the curriculum and the raison d'être of primary schools. Again, the autonomy of primary school teachers in matters of curriculum and pedagogy has been asserted as long-established, unlicensed and unbridled; closer study reveals a curricular and pedagogic conservatism born of an acute awareness of the constraints of political, public and professional opinion and a general unwillingness to risk the educational life-chances of children by undue experimentation. A previous section of this book (Chapter 4) has laid bare the myth of a 'primary school revolution'; a third example of comment that is not based on a knowledge of the realities in schools and classrooms. Many other examples could be cited whose validity could and should be re-assessed in the light of historical research.

Over the last 150 years, the primary curriculum has undergone a series of changes. The term 'changes' is important; talk of the 'development' or 'evolution' of the curriculum is misplaced since such characterization presupposes an end-point to which the changes have contributed or, at the very least, a consistent direction which they embody. No such end point, no such overall direction, no such evolutionary trend, no such 'progress' is discernible. The three types of curriculum analysed here and the fourth type embodied in the National Curriculum (discussed later in Chapter 11) do not represent successive stages but rather embody different conceptions of what the curriculum should be. Despite New Labour's millenarian pretensions, current proposals for reshaping the primary curriculum in terms of a redefined — even more closely specified — 'core', along with a state-approved apparatus of numeracy and literacy 'hours', do not build on past 'best practice' in a cumulative, progressive way, nor do they necessarily represent retrogression from some previous ideal state. They simply present another conception of what the primary curriculum should be, contestable like the other four types discussed here and later in Chapter 11.

is chapter traces changes to the English primary curriculum over a period of 120 years — from the state's first intervention into the curriculum in 1862 to the eve of the introduction of the National Curriculum in 1988. Its focus is on the 'official' curriculum promulgated by central government, and, to a lesser extent, on its implementation in practice. The analysis is conducted in terms of a number of features: a) the nature and extent of legal prescription; b) the rationale (if any) offered for the curriculum; c) its contents in broad terms; d) its assessment; e) its monitoring/ enforcement; f) its susceptibility to change; and g) the extent of its implementation in practice. Based primarily on the nature of the legal prescription underpinning the curriculum, three different curricula are distinguished and their main features characterized.

The 'Payment by Results' Curriculum 1862–97

Until 1870 public elementary education in England was provided by voluntary agencies, very largely the churches, with some financial support from central government from 1833 onwards. In 1862, central government took direct control over the curriculum by dividing elementary education into six stages or standards and prescribing a syllabus in reading, writing and arithmetic for each standard. Those three areas, plus plain needlework for girls, were made compulsory for all schools wishing to attract government grant. All such schools had to be connected with some recognized religious denomination or, at the very least, provide, in addition to secular instruction, 'daily reading of the scriptures'. The government did not prevent schools from offering other subjects but neither did it require them to do so. Infant schools catering for children under 6 were not subject to central control. In reality the government legally prescribed the totality of the curriculum in most elementary schools except for religious instruction. Its legal basis was a 'Revised Code of Minutes and Regulations of the Committee of the Privy Council on Education' (The Revised Code). This code was passed by Parliament but did not constitute an Act or part of an Act of Parliament.

No educational rationale was offered for its introduction beyond the stated object 'to promote the education of children belonging to the classes who support themselves by manual labour'. The immediate aim of the code was to reduce growing government expenditure on public education; in this it was initially successful. It was also introduced to make the content of elementary education more relevant to the needs of contemporary society, rather than simply meeting the needs of the churches. In the view of most educational historians it certainly succeeded in producing an 'orderly, civil, obedient population with sufficient understanding to understand a command' (Tawney, 1924), though whether this was what late Victorian society really needed is more open to question. 'Its further aim was to concentrate the efforts of teachers on the 3Rs (reading, writing and arithmetic) and in this it was partially successful, but only at the cost of forcing entirely mechanical drill methods of teaching on the schools' (Simon, 1965, p. 115).

The initial version of the Code (Appendix A, see p. 64) contained a one-page syllabus which set out the material to be taught in terms of pupils' competencies to be exhibited at an annual examination. No reference was made to the knowledge, understanding or attitudes to be taught to, or developed within, children; pupils were viewed simply as being able (or unable) to demonstrate a limited number of elementary skills devoid of meaning and context. Assessment of competence was assessed annually by the examination of individual pupils by one of Her Majesty's Inspectors; the level of grant awarded to the school and the salary paid the teacher depended largely on the result of this examination. No other form of assessment was prescribed, though in preparation for the inspectors' visit teachers resorted to rehearsing over and over again the answers to the kinds of questions asked by inspectors. The assessment function of the inspectors was combined with a monitoring/enforcement role. Inspectors were able to monitor the effects of the Code on practice in schools through their annual visits; the latter also provided a potent means of enforcing compliance given the link between the annual examination of pupils, the grant payable to the school and the salary paid to elementary school teachers from that grant. In Birchenough's words, as a result of the introduction of the revised Code, 'six cast-iron annual standards were applied to the whole country. The whole arrangement was ridiculously simple, and educational administration was reduced to a mere question of arithmetic. The school became a money-earning institution, and a place for doling out bits of knowledge' (1938, p. 298).

Though rigorously enforced, the curriculum was nevertheless susceptible to change. Gradually the overwhelmingly narrow and utilitarian emphasis of the original Code was modified. Other subjects were made the basis of government grant so that by the 1880s in addition to the original 'elementary' or 'obligatory' subjects there were 'class' subjects such as history, geography and grammar, 'specific' subjects such as agriculture, chemistry and literature, and everyday science in the form of 'object lessons' for standards I–III. Towards the end of the century yet more subjects attracted grants; these included Latin, mechanics, zoology, chemistry, gardening, singing and recitation.

The Victorians were very interested in educational developments elsewhere in Europe; inspectors such as Matthew Arnold reported on their visits to countries such as Prussia and France. There was some evidence of foreign influences: provision for handicrafts was informed by Prussian experience; in many schools a Swedish system of physical training was introduced; school excursions popular in Switzerland found their way into English schools. Infant education was particularly influenced by the views of Froebel — initially in independent infant schools but later in maintained schools through the employment of Froebel-trained or Froebel-influenced inspectors, teachers and teacher-trainers. According to Bramwell (1961), Froebelism also informed developments in the junior standards of some schools — in respect of handwork, brushwork, nature study and local studies.

There is no doubt that the 'payment by results' curriculum had a marked influence on practice. Its rigid reinforcement through the system of annual examinations of pupils (and indirectly their teachers) ensured compliance with its demands. The system was successful, in discouraging initiative and in developing habits of obedience, docility and passivity — in teachers as well as in pupils. In the words of Edmond Holmes (1911), himself one of HM Inspectors of Schools, that 'deadly system of "payment by results" ... seems to have been devised for the express purpose of arresting growth and strangling life, and bound us all, myself included, with links of iron, and had many zealous agents, of whom I, alas! was one' (p. vii). Elsewhere he wrote of the teachers 'who had drilled themselves into passivity and helplessness (pp. 67–8). As far as the central government was concerned there was no significant implementation problem.

The Codified Curriculum 1897–1926

The withdrawal of the 'payment by results' curriculum in 1897 was shortly followed by a wholesale reform of the administration of the English education system involving the establishment of local education authorities (LEAs) and the abolition of school boards. Central government still retained general oversight of the elementary school curriculum — prescribing it in general terms — but decided to leave its more detailed content sufficiently open to enable individual local authorities, schools and teachers to adapt it to local requirements. The legal basis of the curriculum was a series of elementary education codes issued by the Board of Education and mandatory on all elementary schools in receipt of public funds. The 1904 Code reveals the nature and extent of government prescription of curricular content during the first quarter of this century:

> The curriculum, while allowing for local variants, should provide a training in the English language (including speaking, reading, composition, literature); handwriting taught to secure speed as well as legibility; arithmetic including practical measurement; drawing, comprising drawing from objects, memory and brush drawing; the use of ruler and compasses leading to instruction in handicrafts; observation lessons and nature study, including the teaching of gardening to boys; geography, history, music, hygiene and physical training; for girls cookery, laundry work and housewifery, and moral instruction given both directly and indirectly. (quoted in Birchenough, 1938, p. 236)

The curricular discretion accorded schools was circumscribed partly by the background and experience of the teachers, steeped as they were in the relative passivity and conservatism of 'payment by results', partly by public opinion and partly by the publication in 1905 of the Board of Education's *Suggestions for the Consideration of Teachers and Others Concerned in the Work of Public Elementary Schools*. This publication was not intended to impose uniformity of practice but, written largely by HM Inspectors, it reflected 'effective' work as they saw it and was influential in shaping opinion, policy and, to a lesser extent, practice. Though indirectly prescriptive of content by providing detailed guidance on the subjects contained in the Code it did stress the Board's support for teachers to determine their own teaching methods:

The only uniformity of practice that the Board of Education desire to see in the teaching of Public Elementary Schools is that each teacher shall think for himself and work out for himself such methods of teaching as may use his powers to best advantage and be best suited to the particular needs and conditions of the school. Uniformity in details of practice (except in the mere routine of school management) is not desirable even if it were attainable . . . [But it goes on to warn] freedom implies a corresponding responsibility in its use. (Board of Education, 1905, pp. 3–4)

For the first and only time in the history of English elementary/primary education central government provided a worked up rationale for the school and its curriculum (Appendix B, see p. 65) — in terms of strengthening character, developing intelligence, and helping children practically as well as intellectually for 'the work of life'. It stressed the importance of skills such as observation, clear reasoning and language 'as an instrument of thought and expression'; the need for knowledge of, for example, history, literature, and the 'laws' of nature and health; and the development of attitudes such as 'lively interest', industry, self-control, perseverance and loyalty. Though in large measure rhetorical this rationale did provide elementary schools with broad goals and values towards which to work.

There was one other important, and developing, influence which affected the school curriculum at this period. In 1907 the first steps were taken to permit substantial numbers of pupils from elementary schools to win scholarships to secondary schools at age 11. As a result the junior stage of elementary education in many schools became increasingly examination dominated, particularly as pupils approached the time of the scholarship examination. In Blyth's words 'Instead of the code the scholarship now became the tyrant' (1965, p. 29). The 1904 Code had offered a valuable opportunity for developing more consistent approaches between infant and junior stages but this opportunity was very largely missed.

Apart from the scholarship examination, the assessment of pupils' attainments was conducted internally by the schools. Teachers were encouraged to build 'intelligent questioning' into their 'catechetical' teaching to ascertain how far their teaching had been understood. Examinations, recommended as largely oral for the younger children, were held twice, three times or four times a year. HM Inspectors continued to visit, not primarily to assess the competencies of individual pupils but more to inspect teaching methods, provide an external view of pupils' attainments for teachers and to gather information for the Board as to developments within the system. The fear and trepidation their visits used to inspire in the previous era transferred to the codified curriculum; inspectors remained powerful de facto enforcers of official policy.

There was evidence (Bramwell, 1961) of slow but gradual change in curricula and syllabuses. More emphasis was given to oral work in English; practical arithmetic was gradually introduced; history became more widely taught; nature study, accompanied by gardening, developed rapidly; there was a widening in the scope of art, handwork and physical training; a minority of elementary schools made greater use of activity methods, including drama, with older children.

Blyth argues that the impact of Dewey's view on elementary practice was undeniable. 'Projects, co-operative activities and the elimination of subject divisions began to figure in the best and most fortunate elementary schools' (1965, p. 40). Foreign influences remained strongest on the work of infant departments or schools; in addition to Dewey and Froebel, Montessori had a considerable impact on a minority of schools with her emphasis on structured learning, sense training and individualization. However, at the elementary stage, at least, there was less official interest in overseas developments — a stance that was to persist for much of the century.

With the removal of a detailed syllabus and of the annual examination of pupils by HM Inspectors, schools were free to exercise a measure of discretion but in general they did so only gradually and patchily. According to Holmes, writing in 1911, the methods and attitudes engendered by 'payment by results' were lingering long after its abolition in 1897. The scholarship examination also began to provide a constraining influence on practice. There was some change and development but this was a matter of degree, not any major shift. The 'three Rs' of reading, writing and arithmetic remained the staple fare; the majority of the timetabled day was devoted to their study and practice; other subjects were regarded as far less important; the utilitarian working-class orientation of elementary schooling persisted. Elementary education remained conservative.

The Unregulated Curriculum 1926–88

1926–67

In 1926 the existing elementary code was replaced by a much more compact code of regulations. The former code had only prescribed the curriculum in general terms but its successor was even less prescriptive. It simply required that, 'The secular instruction in a school must be in accordance with a suitable curriculum and syllabus framed with due regard to the organization and circumstances of the school or schools concerned' (section 10a). As with earlier codes its issuing was soon followed by a revised version of the *Handbook of Suggestions for the Consideration of Teachers and Others Concerned in the Work of Public Elementary Schools*, published in 1927. This stated that

> It is not possible to lay down any rule as to the exact number of the subjects which should be taken in an individual school. The choice, indeed, cannot in practice be absolutely free. It is in part determined by public opinion as expressing the needs of the community in which the scholars live. Every normal child must acquire the power of speaking his own language, of reading and writing it, and also some knowledge of arithmetic and measurement. Similarly, the importance of hygiene and physical training on the one hand and of moral training, formal or informal on the other, is so great that no-one would propose their omission from the curriculum of an Elementary School. But in selecting other subjects the decision is not always so easy. (Board of Education, 1927, p. 38)

In 1928 the government of the day accepted the main recommendations of the Hadow Report of 1926 which was largely concerned with 'the education of the adolescent' but which also recommended the establishment of a stage or type of education termed 'primary'. Government policy to establish primary education was not accompanied by a readiness to reconsider the content of the primary curriculum. The vague prescriptions of the 1926 Code remained in place; the successor edition of the 1927 *Handbook of Suggestions* published in 1937 and reprinted in 1942 repeated verbatim the words above.

It was not until the passing of the 1944 Education Act that primary education was established by statute as a recognized stage in the national system of education. There was, however, no central prescription of the curriculum except for religious instruction which had to be provided in every county and every voluntary school. The curriculum of individual schools was to be left under the control of local education authorities — which in practice meant that each school was free to determine its own curriculum within the constraints of public and professional opinion and of the ever-more-dominant system of selection for secondary education for pupils aged 11 ('the 11-plus') at the end of the primary stage.

The only rationale offered the new primary stage and its curriculum was an indirect one — through the duty placed on local education authorities 'to contribute towards the spiritual, moral, mental and physical development of the community by securing that efficient education throughout those stages [of primary, secondary and further education] shall be available to meet the needs of the population of their area' (Part II.7). What constituted 'spiritual, moral, mental and physical development' was not spelt out in the 1944 Act nor in accompanying government publications.

Up to 1944 the curriculum in many infant schools consisted of activities related to reading, writing, arithmetic, dramatic play, scripture, art and craft, music, physical training and large-scale construction. In junior schools or classes catering for 7–11-year-olds, 'the curriculum, in the narrow sense of the subjects studied remained almost unchanged [from the previous period]. It included scripture, English, arithmetic, history, geography, art, craft, music, nature study and physical education. It was rare, in the period 1898 to 1944, to find a primary school in which any of these subjects was omitted and any other included' (Central Advisory Council for Education, 1967, p. 190).

Between 1944 and 1967, and especially in the 1960s, curriculum development resulted in considerable changes to the content of the curriculum — at least as recommended by advisers appointed by local education authorities, by members of curriculum development project teams sponsored by the Schools Council (established in 1964) and by HM Inspectors through their visits to schools and in their publications. These changes were epitomized by changes in terminology: mathematics, religious education, science and physical education began to appear in descriptions of the primary curriculum. There were two additions to the curriculum in the period 1944–67: one an additional subject, the other a 'pseudo-subject'. With the sponsorship of the Nuffield Foundation and the encouragement of central and local authorities a growing number of primary schools introduced the teaching of a modern foreign language — particularly during the 1960s.

The 'pseudo-subject' introduced, particularly for the older pupils, was 'intelligence'. With the establishment of secondary education for all in 1944 and the opening up of the grammar schools to many more pupils, there was very strong pressure on primary schools to prepare their pupils very thoroughly for the selection examination at age 11. Though its actual contents varied from local authority to local authority, that examination usually involved the use of standardized intelligence tests and tests in English and arithmetic/mathematics. The coaching of older children to take such tests was widespread. The backwash of that preparation extended to children aged 7–9, or even younger, in some schools. In addition to the selection tests themselves and the practice tests leading up to them, schools used a variety of assessment methods: diagnostic tests, particularly in arithmetic and reading; standardized tests; teacher-devised tests; and end-of-year examinations. In contrast to the period 1862–97 there was no national system for the assessment of the performance of individual pupils but, in an attempt to monitor reading standards over time, the Ministry of Education commissioned large-scale surveys of reading attainment using the Watts-Vernon reading test in 1948, 1952, 1956, 1964 and 1970, and the NS6 reading test in 1955, 1960 and 1970. There was no systematic monitoring or enforcement of the curriculum by HM Inspectors either; they continued to visit schools, occasionally conducting full inspections, but their role was largely an advisory one — to the schools themselves, to the Ministry of Education and, latterly, to the Schools Council and the School Curriculum Development Committee.

Post-war thinking, but far less practice, was influenced by progressive ideas associated with a motley collection of theorists from abroad such as Pestalozzi, Froebel, Dewey, Montessori and Piaget. Methods involving 'activity and experience', later transformed into 'discovery and experience', were more characteristic of infant rather than junior or primary schools but even there, except in extreme cases, did not prejudice the teaching of reading, writing and number. Simon points out that in junior schools, in the later 1940s, activity methods had 'a certain vogue' but their influence on that sector was never marked while the influence of the selection examination loomed large. Apart from the theorists mentioned above there were few direct foreign influences on English primary education during this period; it continued to be rather insular, and insulated from developments in the rest of Europe.

However, for reasons which remain unclear, by the mid-1960s the myth of a primary school 'revolution' along progressive lines had taken hold in the media. This 'myth' proclaimed English primary education to be the 'best in the world' and encouraged, in the late 1960s, a flood of educationists from abroad, especially the United States, anxious to see 'progressive education' in action. Many were disappointed. The 'progressive' rhetoric was far removed from the prosaic nature of most practice — the author's included! In reality, primary education was only just beginning to emerge from the influence of the elementary school tradition: the curriculum remained dominated by the teaching of reading, writing and mathematics (and for some pupils intelligence), though towards the end of the period moves were afoot to widen and liberalize the content of many of the traditional subjects and to organize at least part of the curriculum around topics or themes which drew on and, at their best, interrelated a number of different subjects.

1967 brought no change to the legal requirements placed on primary schools in respect of the curriculum. They were still required to teach religious instruction (though in practice many did not do so) and they were obliged to provide secular education under the control of the local education authority. Since no LEA prescribed the curriculum to be followed in its schools, the latter were free, within the constraints of public and professional opinion, to teach what they thought was most appropriate for their pupils. However, 1967 was important for two reasons: it marked the publication of a major report on primary education (the 'Plowden Report') written by the government-appointed Central Advisory Council for Education; and it signalled the beginning of a major change in primary education occasioned by the move in an increasing number of LEAs to abolish the selection examination at age 11 and replace selective schools by comprehensive secondary schools.

Both the ending of selection and the climate of professional opinion created by the Plowden Report 'freed up' the primary curriculum in very many LEAs; *Towards Freedom of the Curriculum* was in fact one of the sub-headings in the report. Though government appointed, the Council's observations and recommendations had no legal force but were influential, especially in relation to school and class organization and, to a lesser extent, in relation to the curriculum. In respect of the latter the Council stressed that,

> ... children's learning does not fit into subject categories. The younger the children, the more undifferentiated their curriculum will be ... [It went on to point out that] as children come towards the top of the junior school, and we anticipate they will be there till 12, the conventional subjects become more relevant; some children can then profit from a direct approach to the structure of a subject. Even so, subjects merge and overlap and it is easy for this to happen when one teacher is in charge of the class for most of the time ... Yet an expanding curriculum makes great demands on the classteacher ... The work of the oldest children could be shared by a few teachers who, between them, can cover the curriculum. (CACE, 1967, p. 203)

When it came to discuss the possible content of the primary curriculum, the Council resorted to a very largely traditional subject framework comprising: religious education, English, modern languages, history, geography, mathematics, science, art and craft, music, physical education and sex education.

Successive governments in the 1970s and early 1980s did not change the legal basis of the primary curriculum, even though HM Inspectors suggested an alternative formulation in the report *Primary Education in England* (1978). (In the report, HMI analysed the content of the curriculum in terms of: skills and attitudes; language and literacy; mathematics, science; aesthetic and physical education; social studies.) In the 1980s, central government attempted to create an explicit consensus on the content and outcomes of both the primary and the secondary curriculum but without resorting to detailed central legal prescription. It attempted to do this by beginning to publish broadly agreed curricular objectives for the components of the school curriculum but in the event only published one agreed statement of policy — *Science 5–16* (DES, 1985) — which stipulated that, 'Science should have a place in the education of all pupils of compulsory school age, whether or not they are likely to go on to follow a career in science or technology. All pupils should be properly introduced to science in the primary school' (p. 1). By the end of the period 1967–88 the only subjects primary schools were legally required to teach were religious education and science!

Throughout the period there was no accepted rationale for primary education except for the brief statement in the 1944 Act referred to previously. The Advisory Council did tentatively attempt a rationale for the primary school and its curriculum — encapsulated in the purple prose of paragraph 505 of its report:

> A school is not merely a teaching shop, it must transmit values and attitudes. It is a community in which children learn to live first and foremost as children and not as future adults. In family life children learn to live with people of all ages. The school sets out deliberately to devise the right environment for children, to allow them to be themselves and to develop in the way and at the pace appropriate to them. It tries to equalise opportunities and to compensate for handicaps. It lays special stress on individual discovery, on first hand experience and on opportunities for creative work. It insists that knowledge does not fall into neatly separate compartments and that work and play are not opposite but complementary. A child brought up in such an atmosphere at all stages of his education has some hope of becoming a balanced and mature adult and of being able to live in, contribute to, and to look critically at the society of which he forms a part. Not all primary schools correspond to this picture, but it does represent a general and quickening trend.

The Council was mistaken; the trend was neither 'general' or 'quickening'. Its rationale was not widely acted upon and implemented.

Though progressivism was embraced by only a minority of schools, and even then in such a way as not to endanger the teaching of so-called 'basic skills', the removal of selection at age 11 did leave most schools freer than ever before to determine the content of the curriculum. The evidence of the HMI primary survey (DES, 1978) strongly suggests that many schools found it difficult to know how to capitalize on their new-found freedom, especially in the 7–11 age range. They continued to teach English, mathematics and physical education but beyond that there was very considerable variation from school to school. It is not too much of an exaggeration to claim that a kind of curriculum lottery operated. Children received a markedly different curriculum depending on the school they attended and even, within schools, the class of which they were members. This 'laissez-faire' curriculum produced at its best some outstanding work in specific areas of the curriculum, especially the arts — demonstrating the amazing potential of many primary-aged children and the creativity of some of their teachers.

In almost all schools topic or thematic work was adopted as a means of transacting much of the curriculum though most aspects of English and mathematics continued to be taught separately. The content of the curriculum was influenced in some schools as a result of work from national curriculum development projects and, in some cases, local initiatives. Such change tended to be idiosyncratic and localized. More generally the teaching of a modern language disappeared in most LEAs, and towards the end of the period craftwork began to be replaced by craft, design and technology. The period was marked by a lack of 'curricular consistency' (Richards, 1982). By the early 1980s there was concern over these issues; central government encouraged local authorities to develop and implement curriculum policies in an attempt to provide a more consistent curriculum in their schools (both primary and secondary) but such policies were general and were not always com-plemented by detailed curricular guidance. Where such guidance was provided, it was never considered mandatory for schools to follow it.

For the most part, assessment of pupils' progress was also left to individual schools. Testing, both formal and informal, continued but in most cases not on the scale prior to the abolition of selection. Many LEAs instigated their own pro-grammes for monitoring performance, especially in reading, but there was no con-sistent pattern from LEA to LEA. Central government, in an attempt to monitor standards over time, established an Assessment of Performance Unit. Its original brief was to monitor performance across a wide area of the curriculum using light sampling of pupils nationally; in the event its main foci were, inevitably, mathem-atics and English, and, less inevitably, science. Its work was timely, innovative and widely respected; it was beginning to produce reasonably conclusive data when it was closed down consequent on the introduction of the National Curriculum and its testing regime.

Throughout the period there was no systematic monitoring or enforcement of the curriculum. Local authority advisers tended to advise rather than inspect. HM Inspectors continued to visit schools producing one major report (DES, 1978) on the state of English primary education and producing a variety of internal papers, most of which were not published. Inspectors' reports of the inspection of indi-vidual schools were published from 1983 onwards but did not influence the develop-ing national debate about the curriculum. In 1985, HMI began publishing a series of papers, *Curriculum Matters*, which were both influential and controversial for a short time; they were overtaken by events leading to the establishment of a national curriculum. There were no direct foreign influences on primary education during this period but towards the end of it, in the 1980s, HMI did begin to make visits to examine aspects of other educational systems, initially in the secondary sector but later in the primary stage (DES, 1987, 1989).

Viewed in retrospect, the period from 1967 to 1988 was a remarkable one — remarkable for the freedom of discretion legally allowed schools in curricular matters; for the hesitant way that freedom was exercised in many schools; for the superb work of a minority of teachers; and for the government's timidity and slow progress in tackling what was clearly becoming a 'laissez-faire' curriculum. However, throughout, one feature remained constant — the teaching of literacy and numeracy, seen as the core of the curriculum and the raison d'être of the primary school, as it was of its elementary school predecessor.

APPENDIX A: Syllabus

	READING	WRITING	ARITHMETIC
Standard I	Narrative in monosyllables	Form on blackboard or slate, from dictation, letters, capital and small, manuscript	Form on blackboard or slate, from dictation, figures up to 20 Name at sight figures up to 20 Add and subtract figures up to 10, orally, from examples on blackboard
Standard II	One of the narratives next in order after monosyllables in an elementary reading book used in the school	Copy in manuscript character a line of print	A sum in simple addition or subtraction and the multiplication table
Standard III	A short paragraph from an elementary reading book used in the school	A sentence from the same paragraph slowly read once and then dictated in single words	A sum in any simple rule as far as short division (inclusion)
Standard IV	A short paragraph from a more advanced reading book used in the school	A sentence slowly dictated once by a few words at a time, from the same book, but not from the paragraph read	A sum in compound rules (money)
Standard V	A few lines of poetry from a reading book used in the first class of the school	A sentence slowly dictated once by a few words at a time, from a reading book used in the first class of the school	A sum in compound rules (common weights and measures)
Standard VI	A short ordinary paragraph in a newspaper, or other modern narrative	Another short ordinary paragraph in a newspaper, or other modern narrative, slowly dictated once by a few words at a time	A sum in practice of bills of parcels

APPENDIX B: Board of Education, 1904, Elementary Code

Introduction

The purpose of the Public Elementary School is to form and strengthen the character and to develop the intelligence of the children entrusted to it, and to make the best use of the school years available, in assisting both girls and boys, according to their different needs, to fit themselves, practically as well as intellectually, for the work of life.

With this purpose in view it will be the aim of the School to train the children carefully in habits of observation and clear reasoning, so that they may gain an intelligent acquaintance with some of the facts and laws of nature; to arouse in them a living interest in the ideals and achievements of mankind, and to bring them to some familiarity with the literature and history of their own country; to give them some power over language as an instrument of thought and expression, and, while making them conscious of the limitations of their knowledge, to develop in them such a taste for good reading and thoughtful study as will enable them to increase that knowledge in after years by their own efforts.

The School must at the same time encourage to the utmost the children's natural activities of hand and eye by suitable forms of practical work and manual instruction; and afford them every opportunity for the healthy development of their bodies, not only by training them in appropriate physical exercises and encouraging them in organised games, but also by instructing them in the working of some of the simpler laws of health.

It will be an important though subsidiary object of the School to discover individual children who show promise of exceptional capacity, and to develop their special gifts (so far as this can be done without sacrificing the interests of the majority of the children), so that they may be qualified to pass at the proper age into Secondary Schools, and be able to derive the maximum of benefit from the education there offered them.

And, though their opportunities are but brief, the teachers can yet do much to lay the foundations of conduct. They can endeavour, by example and influence, aided by the sense of discipline, which should pervade the School, to implant in the children habits of industry, self-control, and courageous perseverance in the face of difficulties; they can teach them to reverence what is noble, to be ready for self-sacrifice, and to strive their utmost after purity and truth; they can foster a strong respect for duty, and that consideration and respect for others which must be the foundation of unselfishness and the true basis of all good manners; while the corporate life of the School, especially in the playground, should develop that instinct for fair-play and for loyalty to one another which is the germ of a wider sense of honour in later life.

In all these endeavours the School should enlist, as far as possible, the interest and co-operation of the parents and the home in a united effort to enable the children not merely to reach their full development as individuals, but also to become upright and useful members of the community in which they live, and worthy sons and daughters of the country to which they belong.

References

BRAMWELL, R. (1961) *Elementary School Work 1900–1925*, Durham: University of Durham Institute of Education.

BIRCHENOUGH, C. (1938) *History of Elementary Education*, London: University Tutorial Press.

BLYTH, W. (1965) *English Primary Education: Volume Two*, London: Routledge and Kegan Paul.

BOARD OF EDUCATION (1905, 1927) *Suggestions for the Consideration of Teachers and Others Concerned with the Work of Public Elementary Schools*, London: HMSO.

CENTRAL ADVISORY COUNCIL FOR EDUCATION (1967) *Children and Their Primary Schools*, London: HMSO.

DEPARTMENT OF EDUCATION AND SCIENCE (1978) *Primary Education in England: A Survey by HM Inspectors of Schools*, London: HMSO.

DEPARTMENT OF EDUCATION AND SCIENCE (1985) *Science 5–16*, London: HMSO.

DEPARTMENT OF EDUCATION AND SCIENCE (1987) *Aspects of Primary Education in the Netherlands*, London: HMSO.

DEPARTMENT OF EDUCATION AND SCIENCE (1989) *Education in Denmark: Aspects of the Work of the Folkeskole*, London: HMSO.

HOLMES, E. (1911) *What Is and What Might Be*, London: Constable.

RICHARDS, C. (1982) 'Curriculum consistency', in RICHARDS, C. (ed.) *New Directions in Primary Education*, London: Falmer Press.

SIMON, B. (1965) *Education and the Labour Movement 1870–1920*, London: Lawrence and Wishart.

TAWNEY, R. (1924) *Education: The Socialist Policy*, London: Independent Labour Party.

8   The Place of Subjects in the Primary Curriculum: A National Perspective

The place of subjects within the primary curriculum has been widely misunderstood. Subjects are deeply embedded in the distant and more recent past of primary education as well as in contemporary practices. Subjects have never been disregarded for planning purposes, though they are, and have been, sometimes integrated or interrelated for teaching purposes. As this chapter, written in 1990 as a talk, emphasizes, subjects are, and have been, integral to primary organization, policy and practice.

In the late 1980s the proposed introduction of a subject-based National Curriculum aroused considerable opposition in some quarters as contrary to 'good primary practice' or not in tune with 'primary school philosophy'. It was contrasted to approaches based on wide-ranging topics or themes drawing in, and interrelating, a wide range of subjects. In other quarters it was warmly welcomed as a counter to what was seen as woolly-minded policy and practice involving 'a magpie curriculum of bits and pieces, unrelated and ephemeral' and lacking both the structure and progression to be found in a subject-based curriculum. However, both sets of protagonists based their arguments on inadequate knowledge and understanding of contemporary practice, and both failed to acknowledge that separate subject work could be taught in a variety of different timescales, each with advantages and disadvantages in terms of meeting National Curriculum requirements. In reality, subjects were much more engrained in contemporary organization, planning and practice than either the positive or negative rhetoric suggested. In the event the vast majority of primary schools fairly soon found a modus vivendi *with the subject-based National Curriculum as Chapter 10 illustrates — though not in the way either the protagonists or antagonists of wide-ranging topic work advocated.*

The Nature of HMI Judgments

HMI attempt to give independent professional judgments of educational quality. In particular their focus is on questions such as:

- How worthwhile is the education being provided in this primary school, this primary classroom?
- What is it that children are learning?
- What might be done to make the learning more effective, more worthwhile, in the particular circumstances of this particular institution?

When it is said that HMI try to make such judgments as independent professionals, what is meant is that HMI report what they find rather than what others might like them to find, whether those others be HM government, local authorities, or others. These judgments of quality are based on the use and evaluation of evidence. There are three major kinds of evidence. One is 'paper evidence', paper that is produced in schools (schemes, prospectuses, etc). But, clearly, paper intentions may bear very little relevance to experienced reality. So a second level of evidence is 'oral evidence'. HMI talk to teachers, to advisers, to advisory teachers, to heads, to find out what their aspirations are. The third kind of evidence is 'teaching and learning as it happens' — as it is actually observed through extensive classroom observation of children's learning and through interacting with children as they learn. This kind of evidence provides the most significant source of judgments.

In making these judgments of quality, HMI do not have a predetermined blueprint against which to scale or judge each school or classroom. There is no extensive secret list of approved practices expected in every school. For example, the National Curriculum attainment targets and programmes of study are not taken as the sole yardstick by which to judge quality. The worth of what is seen in classrooms is more than the sum total of the presence or absence of particular items, whether or not those items are in the Statutory Orders.

Although there is no blueprint, there is a framework in which evidence is collected and evaluated. The framework comprises sets of criteria against which our professional judgments are made. Such criteria are not usually precisely quantified items — for example, 'Science must take up $17\frac{1}{2}$ per cent of the curriculum in Year 1' — rather they are broad principles which can be converted into questions focusing on what is going on in particular classrooms. For example, there are questions like: 'How far does the standard of work that children are doing in this class match what HMI believe they are capable of doing?' 'How far is the assessment of work in this class consistent or regular and how far does it contribute to the planning of the work?' Such general criteria as these can be applied across the curriculum, across the range of experiences and also, of course, can be applied to particular subjects or areas of the curriculum.

Some criteria are more subject specific. They represent a view of some of the key concepts the children might acquire, through the study of history for example, or what sort of skills they should be developing in art or in music — and these also form part of the criteria.

The criteria, or the principles underlying HMI judgments, then, are built up from the experience of inspecting and are modified and subject to change as a result of that experience, both individually and collectively, through formal and informal discussion within HMI.

To some extent the criteria HMI have used have remained implicit rather than explicit in inspection reports and practice. But the annex to HMI *Primary Education in England* (1978) has a summary of the schedules, the key ideas that were in the inspectors' minds when they made the judgments reported there. The *Aspects of Primary Education* series on history and geography or on early years, for example, has chapters on factors contributing to quality and there some of these criteria are made explicit.

The Place of Subjects in the Primary Curriculum

In making these judgments and reporting them in publications such as *Primary Education in England* or the *Aspects of Primary Education* series, HMI has often used a subject perspective in which to approach matters. It is not true of *Education in the Early Years*, but all the other 'Aspects' documents have tended to use the subject perspective, and this raises the issue of the place of subjects within the primary curriculum. The subject-based framework of the National Curriculum makes this an issue of particular relevance currently, but it is a perennial issue which has been debated with rather more heat than light over the years. There are at least two generalizations about it.

First, subjects, however defined, have long been established as a framework for analysing and describing the curriculum offered to children of primary school age. A subject-based framework, for example, was used by government bodies such as the Board of Education during the early part of this century. The Board of Education Reports over the years, including handbooks of suggestions produced under its aegis, offered, very largely, a subject-based framework for analysing what it was children of elementary school age should be learning. The Ministry of Education, through its document, *Primary Education* 1959, for example, used a subject perspective. The DES, of course, currently uses a subject perspective. The Inspectorate, in its reports, used, to a very large extent, a subject perspective, for example in the National Primary Survey, in the *Aspects of Primary Education* series, in SCI's Annual Report and in the headings which are used very often in describing and analysing the curriculum of individual schools. National committees have tended to use subject perspectives too to some degree. The Hadow Report of 1931 did so. So, importantly, did the Plowden Report, which contained over 50 pages devoted to discussing 'experiences and ideas within the traditional subjects suitable for primary school children'.

Of course, the nature of the subject-based frameworks has changed over time. The names of subjects changed; for example, 'nature study' became 'science'. The content of subjects is constantly being reinterpreted. What the 1927 *Handbook of Suggestions* said was the subject matter of arithmetic or mathematics is different from the Statutory Orders of 1989. But, nevertheless, it is still recognizably the same subject. New subjects are introduced into the analyses — technology is a recent example. Other subjects disappear, largely or as independent entities; gardening, for example. Some subjects even appear and then, very largely, disappear — primary French — perhaps even to reappear again sometime — who knows? As a generalization, there is a long tradition of considering the primary curriculum or the elementary school curriculum in subject terms, despite commonplace rhetoric to the contrary.

The second generalization is an extension of the first one; 'subjects' are intrinsic to contemporary practice and organization in the primary school, and not just because of the advent of the National Curriculum. For example, in their sections related to the curriculum, school prospectuses use recognizable subject terms, subject labels and subject ways of describing the curriculum. Likewise, the policies and schemes of work in primary schools will have recognizable subject labels or titles — mathematics scheme, or PE scheme, or music scheme. There may be documentation on structured play or topic work which may be rather different, but many of the schemes will be recognizably, in a sense, subject ones. The allocation of responsibilities is also frequently for subjects. Of course, there will be other people with broader ranges of responsibility (assessment and evaluation, for example), but responsibilities of teachers are increasingly framed, to some extent at least, in terms of subjects. Teachers' plans and forecasts about what they intend to do or records of what they have done also usually embody a subject frame of analysis.

Perhaps most significantly of all, in view of that third source of evidence mentioned earlier, in classrooms much (not all) of the curriculum transacted, and much of children's learning taking place, is within a 'subject context'. There is, for example, separate teaching of music and PE in primary schools. The issue is not whether this is right or wrong; it is simply a statement of fact. Where RE is explicitly taught it is usually, although not always, separately identified. A large proportion of the mathematics in Key Stages 1 and 2 and of the English work in Key Stage 2 is undertaken separately. Increasingly there is the development of science-focused topics in Key Stage 1. The point of all this evidence is that subjects are actually much more ingrained or embedded in contemporary organization and practice than the rhetoric of primary education would suggest.

A number of questions following from the above points:

a) How is the primary school curriculum best described in order to communicate with parents, governors and others? In particular, what are the advantages and disadvantages of employing a subject-based framework in that act of communication with parents and governors?

b) Secondly, how is the primary curriculum best analysed for planning purposes? — which is a rather different sort of question from that in (a). Again, what are the advantages and disadvantages of a subject frame of analysis there?

c) Thirdly, how is the primary curriculum best transacted with children in classrooms? And, again, what are the advantages and disadvantages of subject-based teaching?

Children's Learning in Subjects

For the sake of analysis it may be taken for granted that 'subjects' are an important aspect of contemporary organization and planning in practice in primary schools, and that HMI are able to apply criteria, both general and subject specific, to assess the quality of children's learning. On this basis, what issues arise from inspections carried out in 1989–90 — the first year of the implementation of the National Curriculum?

a) Firstly, all primary school children have the opportunity to learn what the critics would call 'the basic skills', but the basic skills that primary school children need to learn are more than the basic skills in those three areas normally associated with them. Children experience and learn basic skills across the curriculum; in areas like PE they learn basic skills; in music they acquire basic skills and in science they are learning basic skills as they engage with scientific processes.

b) Beyond that basic curriculum — with a small 'b', not the official Basic Curriculum — there are very great differences among primary schools in terms of the range of learning opportunities provided. Such differences between schools appear more marked in some subjects, such as history and geography, than others, such as PE. Secondly, the variation in the quality of work continues to be very wide, not only from school to school but often, although usually to a lesser extent, within the same school. The best practice continues to extend our knowledge of what primary-aged children are capable of learning in subject terms. It is clear that primary children are capable of understanding ideas, performing operations and engaging in skill development in ways that are far beyond what had been traditionally regarded as appropriate — children are constantly surprising us.

c) The balance of the curriculum continues to demand attention in many schools, with the technological, historical and geographical aspects often requiring greater emphasis. Balance is a problem within subjects too. The question of internal balance is an interesting one — it is arguable that the question of internal balance may be more problematic and more important in relation to other foundation subjects than to the core (although important in the core as well).

d) There is increasing evidence of the use of subject-focused topics, especially in science currently, although we may see others in history and geography in future. Inspection evidence suggests that what Year 1 teachers have been doing in relation to science is a profitable line to pursue, i.e. focusing on a subject or an area of study and drawing up other aspects or subjects only where directly relevant.

e) Clearly there is an underlying lack of confidence in particular areas of the curriculum, such as technology, and in aspects like assessment. Reasonably challenging, but not overwhelmingly challenging, expectations need to be established of the primary teaching profession as, in turn, primary teachers need to encourage reasonable but not overwhelming challenges for their pupils.

f) Differentiation of work continues to be a thorny and, in one sense, insoluble problem. It is a pipedream; it is an impossible goal to differentiate work to suit the individual pupil's needs across the range of the curriculum. Nevertheless, steps can be taken to improve, to some degree, differentiation of work within the limits of the possible rather than the desirable.

g) The last issue relates to children's learning. We do not know enough about children's learning but, largely from professional experience and aided at least to a certain extent by psychological research, we know at least some of the kinds of tasks which make demands on children's thinking and which extend their learning. Inspection evidence suggests that pupils learn most effectively when they are actively involved in tasks which:

  i)   provide first-hand experience involving, for example, manipulative skills, observation, measurement, data collection, analysis and interpretation;

  ii) require recording, reporting or imaginative response using language or other forms of communication;

  iii) demand thought and allow the development and application of knowledge, understanding and skills in contexts or in solving problems;

  iv) involve the use of a range of interesting materials and a variety of approaches;

  v)   require practice of the skills involved in finding out information;

  vi) give responsibility for ensuring that assignments are completed and for producing work of the best possible quality.

The Relevance of the National Curriculum

In conclusion, the National Curriculum is certainly described in subject terms by statute. However, many Key Stage 1 teachers have reminded us through their practice that it does not necessarily have to be enacted in subject terms. But there are advantages and disadvantages in that act of transaction, whether in subject terms or otherwise. It is described in subject terms but, over the years, subjects have been reinterpreted; the subject 'science', for example, which happens to be, at the primary stage, a collection of 14 attainment targets, is in many ways different from the science which would have been found in Plowden or the *Handbook of Suggestions* of 1927, or, for that matter, science as found in many secondary schools. The National Curriculum and the National Curriculum Statutory Orders so far published require children to learn skills associated, to use a composite term, with 'exploration and process', but they also require children to develop knowledge and understanding as well. The National Curriculum Statutory Orders embody many, perhaps most, of the ways in which primary teachers believe children learn. The challenge facing primary schools is to synthesize knowledge and understanding with exploration and process by undertaking tasks which have some of those characteristics listed in the previous section. It is a very demanding challenge and one that cannot be met overnight. In the Inspectorate's view, teachers of children in Year 1 have made a promising start in creating that synthesis. Certainly, key learning processes such as observation, classification, data collection, analysis and so on, are being fostered in a very large number of classes. Knowledge and understanding too are being developed. The kinds of learning tasks outlined previously are being provided in many Key Stage 1 classrooms. Can teachers at Key Stage 2 rise equally to the challenge?

9   The Implementation of the National Curriculum in Primary Schools 1988–93

The design and implementation of the National Curriculum constituted the most extensive curriculum development enterprise this century — greater in scale, even, than the national literacy and numeracy strategies introduced in 1998 and 1999. In its early years, its gradual implementation was monitored by HM Inspectorate and, to a lesser extent, by officers of the National Curriculum Council. Evaluation by independent researchers was far less extensive. The political rhetoric which helped launch the National Curriculum in 1987–88 promised (perhaps even expected) rapid improvements in educational standards and quality and the equally rapid establishment of a consistently implemented curriculum characterized by greatly improved progression and continuity within and between stages.

Inspection evidence of the first four years of implementation from 1989, outlined in this chapter (published originally in 1993), revealed the inevitable gap between fine rhetoric and messy reality. It did, however, report unspectacular but tangible improvements in the breadth, balance and consistency of the primary curriculum; in its overall planning and, to a lesser extent, its assessment; and in standards of attainment in particular subjects, especially science, history and geography. Inspection revealed the difficulties teachers had in coming to terms with both the design technology and information technology components of the statutory orders — problems which remain to this day. It also suggested that some primary schools were beginning to rethink aspects of pedagogy and staff deployment, particularly but not only in Key Stage 2. This reconsideration was being brought about by the increasing difficulties teachers were finding in providing work of appropriate depth and breadth as successive aspects of the National Curriculum came on stream. The manageability issue came to dominate curriculum discussion in 1992 and 1993 and led to the Dearing Review of 1993. The Review retained the overall breadth of the National Curriculum but pared back the detailed content and cut back on the testing requirements, focusing national assessment on 'core' aspects of English and mathematics for 7-year-olds and on English, mathematics and science for 11-year-olds.

Dates

When reflecting on the implementation of the National Curriculum it is easy to forget that it was only as recently as 1989 that requirements in terms of attainment targets and programmes of study became statutory and then only for three subjects and for one year group (Year 1). It is easy to forget that in the school year 1992–93 such requirements do not yet apply at all in Year 6 and only partly apply in Years 4 and 5. It is easy to 'forget' that it will not be until 1996 that the National Curriculum is fully implemented in both Key Stages 1 and 2 and that it will not be until 1999 that children will leave their primary schools having been subject to National Curriculum requirements in all subjects throughout Years 1–6. These key dates 1989, 1996 and 1999 need to be borne in mind as individual teachers and schools appraise their efforts at implementation and as other agencies — be they central government, the School Curriculum and Assessment Authority (SCAA), local education authorities or OFSTED — evaluate progress thus far. Perhaps one further date needs to be added — 2003 — when the first cohort of pupils will complete the first period of compulsory education to have been framed throughout in terms of National Curriculum requirements. Indeed, 1993 may be characterized as just 'beyond the end of the beginning' — a convenient time to take stock, but in a formative, not summative, sense.

Challenges

As primary schools seek to meet the curricular requirements of the Education Reform Act, the challenges they face relate to curriculum, assessment and pedagogy.

For the first time this century primary schools are required to plan and transact curricula framed in very large measure by a legal specification. They have some room for manoeuvre beyond the legal requirements and some opportunity for choice and variation within them, inevitably, given that the curriculum has to be described and analysed in language which is always open to interpretation. Schools are, however, constrained to implement the National Curriculum and to a timescale not of their choosing.

For the first time since the widespread, but not universal, abolition of the '11-plus' examination, primary schools are having to work to an externally prescribed assessment system requiring the administration of tests to particular age groups together with the practice of continuous assessment in the light of externally set criteria. Again, schools have room for manoeuvre and interpretation, given the nature of the language in which assessment procedures and outcomes are described, and given the nature of assessment 'know-how' in many areas of the curriculum. However, the challenges and constraints of assessment requirements are real enough.

Primary schools are also facing a challenge to reconsider their pedagogic and organizational practices — challenges coming from professional, and increasingly from political, sources. Teachers are being asked, *not* required, to review and, where necessary, modify their teaching techniques, the forms of grouping they use, and the way they organize time and content. Here, room for manoeuvre and interpretation is wider, but not limitless. Not every teaching technique is suitable for transacting every aspect of the National Curriculum. The notion of 'fitness for purpose', though not a precise criterion, does rule out the use of particular aspects of pedagogy to meet particular National Curriculum requirements.

Curriculum, assessment and pedagogy are major components of the culture of primary teachers. Attempts at a measure of cultural redefinition are being made, particularly but not only in Key Stage 2; long-held assumptions and long-practised procedures are being challenged; the resilience, as well as the flexibility, of the beliefs and values of many practitioners are being tested.

Curriculum and Assessment

Inspection evidence reveals that the introduction of the National Curriculum is having many beneficial outcomes in teaching and learning. In very many schools, the curriculum is broader than hitherto, at least in outline: in the vast majority of primary schools all nine subjects of the National Curriculum are taught in some form or other, not always in every class, not always to a significant degree, but they are present in the school's curriculum as a whole. The curriculum experienced by the pupils is more consistent: the very wide variation in the content actually taught has been reduced, though wide variations in the standards achieved and in the quality of learning and teaching remain. Many schools provide a more balanced curriculum, though in a large number there is a tendency to concentrate unduly on the core subjects, especially English and mathematics, to the detriment of the other foundation subjects and, particularly, religious education. The introduction of attainment targets has brought greater clarity to the cognitive objectives pursued by primary schools: such targets provide reasonably clear, though not precise, object-ives related to the knowledge, skills and understanding children should acquire in Key Stages 1 and 2. The programmes of study setting out what is to be taught help provide a more consistent national programme of work than previously, when all 19,000 primary schools were able to make individual decisions about content coverage.

Standards of achievement in mathematics and English remain satisfactory or better in about three-quarters of lessons in Key Stage 1 and about two-thirds of lessons in Key Stage 2, though in certain aspects, such as reading standards, they are higher. There have been encouraging signs in some subjects. The introduction of National Curriculum requirements in science, for example, is leading to substanti-ally better standards than hitherto, though too many pupils still make insufficient progress in investigative skills and/or lack an understanding of key scientific ideas. History and, to a lesser extent, geography are now more firmly established in both Key Stages. In history, standards of achievement are better than pre-National Cur-riculum, but many children find difficulty with, or have few opportunities to study, those aspects dealing with interpretations of history and the use of historical sources. The introduction of the Statutory Orders for history and geography has provided opportunities for children to engage in a wider range of more purposeful writing — opportunities exploited in some, but by no means all, schools.

On the other hand, schools have found it very difficult to cope with the range and depth of work envisaged in the original technology Orders and only in a minority have standards of pupils' achievements been satisfactory. Requirements in art, music and physical education have only recently been introduced. It is too early to make firm judgments of the effects on standards in these subjects, though many schools are concerned at their ability to cope with National Curriculum requirements without putting at risk standards elsewhere in the curriculum. This is symptomatic of a more general problem: primary schools are finding it very difficult to 'reconcile' the need to cover the range of work embodied in the programmes of study for all nine subjects with teaching it to an appropriate depth.

The quality of teacher assessment in Key Stage 2 is beginning to improve, albeit from a low base, but is generally much less satisfactory than practice in Year 2 where many teachers have developed considerable expertise. In general, Key Stage 2 teachers are not exploiting the assessment information in the core subjects sent on from the previous key stage to help them plan work for individuals or groups. Teachers have found it very difficult to assess design and technology capability.

Unsurprisingly, few schools have effective systems for assessing attainment in history, geography, art, music or PE at this early stage in the implementation of the National Curriculum in these subjects.

The organization of the primary curriculum is undergoing evolutionary change. Although, as a recent HMI report (OFSTED, 1993, p. 18) points out, 'there is no evidence that large numbers of schools are preparing to jettison topic work as *one* way of organising aspects of the curriculum', many schools are reappraising their approach to topic work. Increasingly, topic work is planned in outline on a whole school or whole key stage basis and involves cycles of topics planned, in many cases, jointly by teachers. Very many schools are making more use of 'subject-focused' topics devised to meet particular National Curriculum requirements. In some cases, schools plan topics but include within them some separately identified and taught subject work. Increasingly some subjects are taught both as part of topics, and separately. The amount of separate subject teaching is increasing, particularly, but not only, in Key Stage 2.

Pedagogy and Staff Deployment

In addition to informing the debate about subject and topic work, the paper *Curriculum Organisation and Classroom Practice in Primary Schools* (Alexander, Rose and Woodhead, 1992) aimed to promote discussion followed by review and, where necessary, change in pedagogy and patterns of staff deployment.

A year or more on from its publication, in all year groups in almost all primary schools, the class-teacher system remains the dominant mode. However, its total dominance is being questioned in a growing number of schools. A significant minority engage in a measure of semi-specialist teaching (that is, class teachers also teach a particular curriculum area to classes other than their own). Such teaching usually involves only a small number of subjects and often involves teachers in exchanging classes for particular 'semi-specialisms'. A small number of schools employ fully specialist teachers, but such staff are almost invariably part-time and only a small number of subjects or aspects of work (for example, music or special needs) are taught in this way. There is strong resistance, on both ideological and logistical grounds, to full-time, fully specialist teaching. There is, however, less resistance to, and a growing recognition of, the importance of semi-specialist teaching, especially in Key Stage 2. Here 'financial limitations, rather than "ideological" objections, are increasingly cited as inhibiting its development' (OFSTED, 1993, p. 19).

It is difficult to know how far the balance between class, group and individual work is changing. In Key Stage 2 there is wide recognition of the value of whole class teaching for specific purposes and there is a greater reported incidence of it in practice. This greater use may be the result in some cases of conscious decision-making by individual teachers or in others of teachers' growing willingness to admit their long-established use of it, now that a more propitious climate for that disclosure exists. Not enough teachers make conscious decisions in the light of an analysis of its potential benefits. Some, for example, continue to employ it indiscriminately, even though it may be 'unfit for purpose'. The organization and teaching of groups remain difficult areas for many primary teachers. Although grouping is a common feature in classrooms, very many of these groups are not taught *in* groups, nor are they given tasks which require them to work collaboratively *as* groups. In too many cases the pedagogic rationale for grouping remains unclear or unanalysed. The same stricture can be applied to individualized work which, in some classes, especially in subjects such as mathematics, is overemphasized so that pupils have few opportunities to benefit from close discussion with their teacher or with other children about the work in hand. *Curriculum Organisation and Classroom Practice in Primary Schools* (Alexander et al., 1992) has helped reinforce the importance of direct teaching techniques such as explaining, questioning and instructing, and the need to create opportunities for these techniques to be used purposefully. The introduction of the Statutory Orders for history and geography has emphasized the importance of rather less widely used direct teaching techniques such as interpretation, prediction or speculation. However, it is important to acknowledge that in pursuit of some attainment targets teachers need to provide opportunities for the pupils *themselves* to explain, question, instruct, define, predict and speculate.

The 1992 discussion paper (Alexander et al., 1992), along with the phased introduction of the National Curriculum has helped instigate a long-overdue debate about pedagogy and organization in primary schools. The advantages and disadvantages of particular teaching methods, grouping practices, and patterns of staff deployment are being discussed in a growing number of schools. In the future, perhaps, the term 'pedagogy' itself may well become established as part of the professional vocabulary of primary school teachers.

Depth, Breadth and Manageability

Of the host of curriculum issues raised by the introduction of the National Curriculum the problems of breadth, depth and manageability are of particular importance at the present time. Although all nine subjects of the National Curriculum are taught in some form or other in the vast majority of primary schools, teachers, particularly but not only in Key Stage 2, are meeting substantial difficulties in teaching the programmes of study to the required depth, whether they teach subjects separately or as part of topics. They have found it difficult enough with the three core subjects; most have found it impossible with technology, hence the revision to the technology Orders themselves. Many teachers are daunted by the demands of the history and geography Orders and feel that coverage is likely to be secured only at the expense of depth. In particular, schools with mixed-age classes are experiencing particular problems with the coverage of history study units; gaps or repetition have frequently resulted. This problem of the reconciliation of depth and breadth of work is likely to intensify as schools attempt to implement attainment targets and programmes of study in music, art and PE. The issue is at the heart of the manageability problem.

Such difficulties may sometimes be partly the result of weaknesses in curriculum planning and organization but they often originate in the nature of the National Curriculum requirements themselves. Currently, for example, teachers in Year 5 have to meet Key Stage 2 requirements which involve them planning, transacting and assessing a curriculum which comprises:

- over 30 attainment targets;
- over 400 statements of attainments;
- over 50 closely set pages of programmes of study;
- Statutory Orders structured in a variety of different ways and with attainment targets and programmes of study presented in a variety of formats.

In addition there is the expectation, unreasonable or otherwise, that the curriculum they provide will be adapted to the capabilities of individuals and groups within the class. This excludes the teaching of religious education (another statutory requirement) and teaching related to cross-curricular issues.

A recent OFSTED report (1993, p. 20) states that: 'The difficulties schools face in reconciling adequate depth and breadth in the curriculum ... provide a powerful reason for arguing that the requirements of the whole curriculum, including the National Curriculum, should be reappraised, not hurriedly but in a measured way, taking particular account of the practice of those primary schools which have coped relatively successfully with the implementation of the National Curriculum thus far.'

Taking Stock

The culture of primary education, as it is embodied in the beliefs, assumptions and practices of many teachers, is being challenged: the introduction of the National Curriculum into Key Stages 1 and 2 is part of that challenge. Cultures do not change overnight. Nor, if they are healthy, do they remain the same when the surrounding environment changes radically. The culture is changing. The introduction of the National Curriculum is leading to changes and improvements in the curriculum experienced by pupils. However, the degree of change and improvement should not be overstated. There is still much to do if the full range of curricular requirements of the Education Reform Act are to be well met at the primary stage. However, at this time of stock-taking, it is important for schools, and for individual teachers, to review and appreciate how far they have come since 1989 as well as being, as many are, all too conscious of how far they still have to go.

References

ALEXANDER, R., ROSE, J. and WOODHEAD, C. (1992) *Curriculum Organisation and Class-room Practice in Primary Schools*, London: DES.

OFSTED (1993) *Curriculum Organisation and Classroom Practice in Primary Schools: A Follow-up Report*, London: OFSTED.

10 The Implementation of the National Curriculum in Small Primary Schools 1989–97

It is surprising that there has been no large-scale evaluation of the implementation of the National Curriculum ten years since its introduction in 1989. In its very early stages, progress was monitored through the work of HM Inspectorate, but with the creation of OFSTED in 1992 HMI's activities were refocused on setting up and regulating the new independent inspection system and training inspectors to operate the framework for inspection. Since then, OFSTED inspections of individual schools have not really focused on the extent to which National Curriculum requirements have been implemented or the successes and problems schools have had with those changing requirements. Nor has the limited amount of HMI's own inspection activity been directed to those sorts of issues. Admittedly the National Curriculum Council and its successor, the School Curriculum and Assessment Authority, have engaged in monitoring work but their efforts have been constrained by limited staff and resources and have not focused on the observation and evaluation of the curriculum as taught in classrooms and experienced by the children. The limited amount of independent academic research has not had that focus either. The absence of a systematic comprehensive evaluation is very regrettable given the vast amounts of money, time and energy expended on National Curriculum implementation. As a consequence, suggested revisions to the curriculum have not been based on adequate evidence of what is happening 'at the chalkface', and critics of primary education (and of the National Curriculum itself) have been able to make unsubstantiated claims which cannot easily be countered.

The limited evidence available suggests that in general the implementation of the National Curriculum in primary schools has been a qualified success and has brought about valuable, though unspectacular changes in the ways in which the curriculum is planned, organized, taught and assessed. Chapters 8, 9 and 11 include general overviews based on my reading of the limited evidence available.

This particular chapter, written in 1998, has limitations: it focuses on small primary schools only; on Key Stage 2 only; and on 13 schools only. It illustrates what it describes as the confident 'domestication' of the National Curriculum in the small schools studied and suggests that similar processes and outcomes might be at work more generally, though not universally.

Introduction

In terms of implementing the National Curriculum, small primary schools tend to be seen as 'deficit systems'. *Curriculum Organisation and Classroom Practice in Primary Schools* (Alexander et al., 1992) neatly characterizes the 'common sense', all too often taken-for-granted, view that with limited curricular (especially subject) expertise at their disposal small schools' ability to 'deliver' the National Curriculum is problematic: 'There is . . . the *problem* of the small school, where it is unreasonable to expect that two or three teachers can be expert in ten subjects to the depth now required' (para. 79, my italics). And again later in paragraph 150: 'It is as wrong to assume that a small school cannot meet the full range of requirements of the National Curriculum as it is to assume that a large school can, *but the balance of probability tends that way*' (my italics). That all seems intuitively very reasonable but reality in education can sometimes appear, or be, counter-intuitive. There is, for example, extensive unpublished evidence from OFSTED inspections to support the view that standards of attainment, standards of teaching and standards of learning are rather higher in schools with fewer than 100 pupils on roll than in larger schools, and also *some* inspection evidence that in both Key Stages 1 and 2 small primary schools are rated rather more favourably than larger ones in respect of: a) the content, breadth and balance of the curriculum; and b) curriculum planning and organization.

How far such differences are statistically significant is unknown; OFSTED has not published this data or the degree of its statistical significance. How far such differences are due to socio-economic factors or smaller class sizes is equally unknown. But the OFSTED data is suggestive. It does imply that 'common-sense' ideas of curriculum viability and coverage in small schools bear re-examination and that explanations should be sought which might go some way to explaining apparently counter-intuitive results.

The investigation on which this paper is based attempted to examine the reality (as opposed to the rhetoric) of small schools' planning and implementation of revised National Curriculum requirements in Key Stage 2 with a view to suggesting reasons for the apparent 'better' performance of such schools, at least as judged by OFSTED inspectors.

The investigation, carried out between May 1996 and March 1997, was of provision and practice in 13 small primary schools in a county containing a relatively high proportion of such schools. The sample of schools in the study was chosen on the basis of their staff being known by LEA advisers to take a considered response to the revised National Curriculum requirements. They were not necessarily schools exhibiting 'good practice' (however defined). The schools ranged in size from 36 to 82 pupils on roll; the pupil–teacher ratios varied from 17.1:1 to 25.7:1. All had either two or three classes; usually, though not in every case, the headteacher took the Key Stage 2 class or, less often, a 'transition' class straddling Key Stage 1 and Key Stage 2. In each case the school was in a rural area, usually drawing children from families engaged in farming and other rural or professional occupations.

The methodology employed was a combination of structured observation of the curriculum 'in transaction', scrutiny of documentation and in-depth discussion of policy and practice with the Key Stage 2 teacher. An aide-mémoire was used as an initial focus for discussion and observation. A report summarizing the study's findings was sent back to each school for comment.

Implementation of the Revised National Curriculum

As far as a series of limited visits could ascertain, the revised National Curriculum at Key Stage 2 was generally being implemented confidently and effectively, very effectively in some cases. The National Curriculum was being 'domesticated' to suit the particular circumstances of individual schools. It was not regarded as a threat, nor uncritically as an unqualified benefit. There remained some doubts as to its manageability, very considerable doubts as to the extent of so-called 'discretionary time' and some anxieties about the effects of proposed future revisions. Partly because they were personally teaching it daily, heads and other Key Stage 2 teachers felt confident in meeting its broad requirements and felt comfortable in interpreting its detailed requirements with a degree of flexibility, taking advantage of the generality and ambiguity inherent in the language of the programmes of study.

About a third of the schools were providing a *legal entitlement curriculum* — teaching their pupils the so-called 'basics', the ten subjects of the National Curriculum, and religious education (locally determined). The remaining two-thirds were offering, to varying degrees, an *enriched legal entitlement curriculum* — giving their pupils their legal entitlement in terms of National Curriculum subjects and religious education but going beyond these to offer in 'discretionary time' new subjects, new activities, cross-curricular themes or extension work in existing National Curriculum subjects. None of the schools were reacting to current pressures by reverting to a *neo-elementary curriculum*, involving disproportionate amounts of time devoted to the 'basics' of mathematics and English, and to Key Stage 2 science, and providing only a rudimentary, superficial coverage of other subjects. There was, however, evidence of a small number of teachers wondering whether rather more time than previously should be devoted to English and number skills.

Curriculum Policies

The formulation and review of curriculum policies were firmly established in all the schools and documented in development plans. Partly with OFSTED inspection requirements in mind, the vast majority of the schools had policies in place for all National Curriculum subjects and religious education (though less often for one or more cross-curricular themes), but many acknowledged that due to time constraints on their already hard-pressed small staffs some policies were in need of review.

Most schools were clear as to when, on a rolling programme, those reviews were planned to take place. Most schools had devised their own policies, usually statements of general principle and not reflective of the specific circumstances of individual contexts. There was some evidence of increasing 'personalization' as reviews were proceeding. A small number had been party to the joint production of policies by clusters of schools or, as in one case, had 'bought in', without adaptation, commercially produced statements. It was rare to find policies written to a common format or for them to cover all of the following elements: aims, organization, planning, teaching methods, assessment and recording, and links with other subjects. Only one school had felt confident enough *not* to have produced policies in four subjects until the staff had examined their current practice in each subject, established common goals and language, considered issues of continuity and progression and trialled a draft policy.

It was possible to distinguish three kinds of policies. Some were *rhetorical*, produced out of a sense of duty, obligation or necessity, but offering little more than ritualized phrases and exhortations. Some were *reflective*, providing an explanation and description of current practice. Many, however, were *enabling*, reflecting current practice to some degree but going beyond to provide realistic aspirations for its development. Most schools had examples of all three kinds; some were taking advantage of the review process to produce more of the third type.

Schemes of Work

None of the schools had been able to produce a set of their own individual schemes of work for all subjects by providing detailed breakdowns of the content and activities to be addressed in particular year groups. This was partly because of understandable time pressures on staff, most of whom carried multiple curricular responsibilities, and partly because of the possibly less justifiable view that such detailed schemes were an unnecessary duplication given the comprehensive long- and medium-term planning in place. Two schools, however, had been part of a group who, in collaboration with an LEA adviser, had produced a set of clearly structured schemes of work related to an agreed series of topics. These schemes indicated the topics to be studied in each Key Stage, listed the knowledge and skills to be covered, provided appropriate National Curriculum level descriptors and gave examples of appropriate activities at each level. Though not involved in the production of such schemes, staff in one of the schools who had adopted them felt that they were a welcome aid to planning but retained the right to modify them. A small number of schools had produced brief developmental schemes listing activities to be provided year group by year group in subjects such as art or music or had documented in summary form progression in skills such as handwriting, spelling and geographical enquiry. Some use was being made of 'customized' commercially produced schemes of work for PE.

Planning

In general the schools were characterized by curriculum planning of good quality which was closely and explicitly related to National Curriculum requirements. To facilitate long-term planning, all adopted topic cycles usually focused on themes related to the programmes of study for history, geography and science. The timescales for these cycles varied from one to four years depending either on the nature of the subject (science, for example, was usually based on a two-year cycle, history on four years) and/or on the age range of the classes (four years for classes spanning the whole of Key Stage 2, three-year cycles for classes of children aged 8–11, etc.). Subject to review in the light of experience almost all the schools envisaged retaining the same cycle of topics 'the second time around', though in one case where the same two-year cycle operated for each of the three classes in the school it was intended that the topics be changed at the end of each cycle. In almost every case, broad mapping against programmes of study had taken place. While most schools had devised their own cycle, three had adopted sets of topics with other neighbouring schools. The limitations of topic cycles were readily acknowledged, especially the difficulty of avoiding some elements of repetition or omission over long periods, the differential depth of coverage depending on the age at which children met particular topics, and the difficulties in terms of continuity and progression of experience for individual pupils as they transferred in and out of small schools. Mathematics and English rarely featured as main areas in the topic frameworks but were often cited as areas requiring work on a continuing basis, though they sometimes featured as making contributions to specific topics.

Many, though not all, of the schools had agreed procedures and formats for medium-term planning, usually on a half-termly or termly basis. Topics or themes (particularly science-focused ones) were most often planned on the first of these timescales, though in some classes single topics might last the whole of a term or major and minor ones might run concurrently over that period. In all cases, the contribution of individual subjects to topics was identified and analysed. Some schools adopted different formats and planning timescales for thematic work and for non-thematic work such as number, spelling, handwriting, physical education and music. Most plans were impressively thorough in terms of the provision of activities (very often interesting and sometimes differentiated by level), their cross-referencing to the statutory orders and the resources required to implement them. A majority were characterized by reasonably clear learning intentions but in fewer were assessment opportunities identified in any detail, cross-curricular themes referred to, or regular reviews/evaluations provided. Copies of medium-term plans were usually stored centrally for use in planning topics 'the second time around' or in helping teachers decide on what more challenging work to provide for children as they move through the school.

Few of the schools had agreed procedures for short-term planning on weekly or daily timescales. These plans varied widely in content and detail and rarely made learning objectives explicit; some were little more than working notes or jottings.

Nevertheless the learning activities seen were usually appropriate, sometimes differentiated and evoked positive responses from the children.

Curriculum Management

In almost all cases, heads perceived themselves as whole school curriculum coordinators (though not using that exact terminology). They felt able to 'keep a finger on the pulse' of the curriculum through instituting agreed procedures for long- and medium-term planning and through teaching at firsthand all or most of the curriculum. There was surprisingly little systematic scrutiny of colleagues' medium-term or short-term planning, though one school had instituted topic review meetings midway through the term to monitor progress and suggest modifications to plans. Most heads accepted in principle the importance of their role in monitoring and evaluation of colleagues' work but because of lack of non-contact time could not provide this except as part of the formal process of appraisal or when their classes were taken by student teachers.

Responsibilities for particular subjects were 'carved up' amongst the staff, including, in some cases, part-timers. The 'official' responsibilities for each of their several or many subjects involved course attendance, resource management, advice on planning and, prominently, leading the development and review of policy statements. Given the heavy load of such responsibilities on very few staff and the absence of non-contact time, most teachers remained very largely 'dormant coordinators' for most of their subjects most of the time, and only became 'activated' for particular reasons, e.g. when one of their subjects became the focus for a policy review. This tacit acceptance of a degree of *curriculum dormancy* was an understandable and functional response to the range of unrealistic demands too often made of coordinators in small primary schools.

Curriculum Organization

All the schools claimed to organize their curriculum in terms of a combination of topic work and separate subject work, though in one case closer examination revealed a curriculum organized and taught along separate subject lines with only marginal interconnections between areas of study. At Key Stage 2 the vast majority of topics were either *subject-focused* (i.e. concentrating on one subject and drawing on only a limited number of others where these were directly relevant, such as a study of the Victorians which also involved investigation of steam power in design technology and appreciation of paintings in art), or, very often, *subject-specific* (i.e. comprising content and activities within only one programme of study, such as topics on electricity, light, St Lucia). In a smaller number of cases, topics drew equally on two subjects; for example, a project on orienteering involving aspects of physical education and geography. In contrast to the situation in Key Stage 1, few topics (e.g. pattern, change, the local area) were *broad-based* and drew on a wide variety of subjects. No opportunities were provided for children to pursue *divergent* topics where starting from a common point pupils, individually or in groups, pursued topics of their own with the teacher facilitating rather than directing the work. In some classes, children were given some encouragement to pursue different lines of enquiry within the same topic but very much under the teacher's control and direction. With the introduction and implementation of the National Curriculum, the distinction between topic work and separate subject work was being blurred; the dichotomy between subject and topic work was too simplistic to reflect the complexity of curriculum practice in the 13 schools.

Separate subject work took a variety of forms. Skill elements of subjects such as mathematics and English (reading, 'scheme-based' maths, 'quick' maths) were taught separately on an ongoing daily basis, though use was made of these skills in other work. Subjects such as physical education, music and, in many of the schools, religious education were taught regularly, separately, and less frequently over the period of a week. Through the medium of separate 'subject-specific' topics, schools taught aspects of subjects (e.g. pattern in mathematics, magnetism or astronomy in science) on a modular basis. There appeared to be a developing tendency to teach art and design technology partly 'in their own right' and partly to service other work. There was no evidence of classes concentrating entirely or almost entirely on one particular subject for a limited period, e.g. technology or art workshop 'days'. Interconnections and interrelationships between areas of study were facilitated by the use of generalist teaching for most subjects.

There appeared to have been a substantial shift towards more subject-based work since the introduction of the National Curriculum but in no schools were there any plans to make further major changes to the balance of subject and topic work, despite pressures from national sources to do so. The schools had established a *modus vivendi* in relation to the subject basis of the National Curriculum. Heads and other Key Stage 2 teachers felt reasonably confident that their 'mixed economy' was able to 'cover' the relevant elements of the programmes of study, though, in practice, 'covering' might mean 'touching very lightly' on some of these. Very few schools had made conscious, explicit decisions to treat some aspects of the programmes of study more lightly than others.

Discretionary Time

The introduction of the revised orders had led to changes, rarely major ones, in almost all of the schools. Only one had taken 'official' sources at their word by assuming that 20 per cent of discretionary time had been found and planning accordingly. Most heads found it difficult to identify from where they were finding extra time, but with one exception all were exercising a measure of discretion. Three schools, in particular, were very clear as to their use of discretionary time. One school planned to devote more explicit attention to personal and social education (PSE) (including sex and drugs education); to introduce a health education study into each class's topic cycle; and, interestingly, to spend more time with children discussing their 'meta-learning' of mathematics and English. A second school planned swimming for all Key Stage 2 pupils; basic French for Year 5–6 pupils; more investigational work in science; and more environmental education including revising the school's published guide to the local area. A third had increased the time devoted to physical education and had enriched the curriculum in mathematics and music well beyond National Curriculum requirements. PSE, health education, French, drama and more work in the locality or with the community featured as part of discretionary time in one or more of the other schools. Only one school had deliberately re-introduced a broad-based topic, and none had plans for 'divergent' topics. There was little evidence of the schools devoting 'discretionary time' to the further practice and consolidation of literacy and numeracy. Most of the schools had not been able to give thought to longer term curriculum developments, though two were hoping to undertake higher order work in information technology, one as a result of a link with NCET. Overall the introduction of the revised orders had led to teachers feeling rather less pressurized over 'coverage' and rather more willing to take advantage of learning opportunities as they arose incidentally or as had been planned outside National Curriculum requirements.

Curriculum Continuity and Progression

In every case, curriculum continuity and progression with receiver secondary schools were not planned for explicitly. There were some isolated short-term initiatives concerned, for example, with the teaching of AT1 in science, the scrutiny of National Curriculum test papers in Key Stages 1–3 and 'some' discussion of the SCAA Key Stage 2/3 continuity document. In two cases, older pupils received some tuition in aspects of physical education at a local secondary school. The very real obstacles obstructing progression across phases were acknowledged but the implications were not being confronted: either an unprecedented degree of joint planning (and, ideally, teaching) across Years 6–7 or 5–8 (to be ruled out on grounds of impracticability in most contexts) or the systematic use of a common (nationally or locally prescribed?) series of texts/learning materials across those year groups, or a recognition that the problem is insoluble except for a little progress 'at the margins' and therefore problematic in terms of the time and energy needing to be expended.

Pedagogy

The teaching seen was generally both 'fit for purpose' and 'fit for persons'. To use OFSTED-speak, the quality of teaching was satisfactory or better in almost 90 per cent of the lessons, including two-fifths where it was judged good or very good. In every case, mixed-age classes were being taught; and in almost every lesson the teacher was operating as a generalist, not a specialist.

Contrary to the views of some national pundits, the teachers used direct teaching in a variety of contexts. Classes were sometimes taught as a whole, particularly as a prelude to writing, as part of work in physical education, or to introduce or revise topics in subjects such as mathematics. In almost every case work was then differentiated in terms of content or in terms of teachers' expectations (sometimes, but not always, effectively communicated to individuals or groups of pupils). Children also received teaching in small groups: this was often well focused and matched to the similar abilities evident in the group. At other times pupils were taught as individuals; the small size of classes facilitated that kind of interaction, though on occasion the quality of the teaching was adversely affected by its short duration. A high proportion of teachers' time was spent in direct teaching; well-established routines, firm expectations of task-focused behaviour, and acceptance by the pupils of a measure of responsibility for their own learning freed most teachers from the need to supervise, to discipline children or to provide resources while the lesson was in progress and enabled them to devote much of their time to helping individuals or groups learn.

Plenty of examples were seen of teachers employing techniques such as instructing, demonstrating, explaining, describing and questioning, often of a high order but sometimes unnecessarily truncated by the desire to set off children 'working' on paper. Less frequently seen techniques involved teachers in previewing work, setting up role play situations, reviewing and evaluating work or lessons, and probing children's thinking in depth. In most of the lessons children responded very positively and enthusiastically, especially to challenging teaching.

Pupil Grouping

All of the schools formed classes according to pupils' ages; in only rare circumstances, usually where they were of exceptional ability, were children placed other than with their year group. Because of their small size, the schools were not able, had they wanted, to set by ability in subjects across classes in any year group, nor had any considered setting in subjects across mixed-age classes to form, for example, two sets for mathematics, each comprising children in Years 3–6.

In contrast, the use of some form of ability grouping within Key Stage 2 classes was common, though there was no indication that its incidence had increased recently as a result of pronouncements from DfEE or OFSTED. For the most part, teachers' flexible and partial use of similar ability groups was proving beneficial. Spelling and aspects of grammar were often taught to groups of similar ability as was 'computational' (but not always 'topic') mathematics. Ability groups for reading were becoming more common. Pairs of children of similar ability sometimes worked together in IT; it was rare, though not unknown, for ability grouping to be used in science and DT. For aspects of work many schools differentiated by age; for example, in one class the same science-specific topic was taught at one level for pupils in Years 3–4 and at another for those in Years 5–6, with children of similar ability in each group working in pairs. The complexity of internal organization was illustrated in one class where children were grouped by ability for grammar and, separately, for spelling; undertook individual work in number reinforced by some regular teaching in ability groups; pursued class-based 'topic' mathematics; and usually worked in mixed ability pairs or groups in science, though on occasion higher attainers were grouped for investigations at level 5. Except for 'scheme-based' mathematics in some schools there was little sign of individuals (other than those with special educational needs) working on individualized programmes of work. Only two of the schools had plans to review their use of ability grouping; both were considering extending it somewhat.

Staff Deployment

In general the schools were making effective and flexible use of the subject expertise of their staff and were giving Key Stage 2 pupils the opportunity to be taught by more than their own class teacher. The use of semi-specialist teaching was a marked feature — paradoxically, more so than in most medium-sized or large primary schools. Apart from the use of generalist teaching for much of the curriculum, a variety of models of staff deployment were in operation. Teachers exchanged classes for particular subjects — both within Key Stage 2 where, in one case, religious education and physical education were the two subjects involved, or across Key Stages where, in one case, a Key Stage 1 and a Key Stage 2 teacher taught games to children in the opposite Key Stage, or, as in another, where a Key Stage 1 teacher took the headteacher's Key Stage 2 pupils for science while the head took the younger children for activities related to listening, speaking and drama. One school operated a more complex arrangement where once a week the three class teachers engaged in semi-specialist teaching of either art, music or drama, with each of the three classes in the school having 1.5 terms of specialist teaching in each of the two subjects not taught by their class teacher. In several schools the heads contrived to teach all the children at some point or other during the week, sometimes exchanging with, and sometimes working alongside, the class teachers.

Effective use was made of part-time teachers. A number were employed as specialist teachers of music throughout the school; one, for example, spent 20 minutes a week with Year R, 45 minutes with Years 1–2, 80 minutes with the Key Stage 2 class and 30 minutes with the whole school for singing and hymn practice. Some part-time teachers were bought in to give the head time for administration and took either a variety of subjects or, less often, some self-contained work in a single area of the curriculum such as a history study unit. In two cases, part-timers were used to create smaller classes for the teaching of core subjects; in one of these schools the two classes were divided for most mornings into three groups for mathematics and later into three differently constituted groups for English — an arrangement which appeared to be working well. Part-time staff were also used to teach children with special educational needs. Some schools supplemented staff expertise by buying in coaching skills from instructors; by employing consultants for limited periods (for example, to work on Logo and control technology for a morning a week over a half-term block); by using the services of retired or unemployed teachers; and, in a number of cases, by the use of artists who were often able to influence the work of the whole school through even a short time 'in residence'.

Most of the schools were satisfied with their balance of generalist and specialist teaching. None had plans to dispense or reduce the incidence of the latter. Two were planning to increase it: one by employing a part-time specialist teacher for information technology for half a day a week, and the other to provide specialist teaching of art and physical education through a weekly exchange involving the two Key Stage 2 teachers. Overall the use of both generalist and specialist teaching to help provide a balanced and appropriately challenging curriculum in Key Stage 2 was a striking feature of most of the schools in the survey. Flexible patterns of staff deployment were the norm, not the exception. They were the result of considered reflection on the most effective use of the staff expertise available, not knee-jerk reactions to outside criticisms of the class teacher system in primary schools.

Moving Forward

The schools in the survey were not necessarily representative of small rural primary schools in that particular county or nationally. Irrespective of their degree of representativeness, they displayed a range of positive features which may go some way to explaining unpublished findings from OFSTED inspections in which small schools (defined arbitrarily as having fewer than 100 pupils on roll) have been judged rather more favourably than larger ones in terms of children's standards of attainment, the quality of teaching and the quality of learning. Some of these features were 'givens' and not directly attributable to the staffs of the schools: the small number of children on roll; smaller class sizes; and the nature of the intake, often comprising a mixture of children from well-established farming families and from professional ones. Many, however, were directly attributable to the professionalism of the staff: the confident 'domestication' of the National Curriculum; its selective enrichment; medium-term planning of generally good quality; non-doctrinaire approaches to curriculum organization involving a mixed-economy of topic and subject work; an eclectic pedagogy fit for both 'purpose' and 'persons'; in-depth knowledge of children; the sensible use of ability grouping; and flexible patterns of staff deployment involving a measure of semi-specialist teaching. Not all the schools exhibited all these features; many did. On a national scale, many small primary schools do.

Reference

ALEXANDER, R., ROSE, J. and WOODHEAD, C. (1992) *Curriculum Organisation and Classroom Practice in Primary Schools*, London: DES.

11   The Primary Curriculum 1988–99

The primary curriculum is currently (1999) in a curious, unstable and intermediate state. Many of its statutory elements have been suspended at least to the year 2000 to enable schools to concentrate on an ITEMS-based curriculum (ICT, English, mathematics and science). There is a particular drive to implement national literacy and numeracy strategies which constitute central government's most direct and comprehensive 'incursion' into what primary teachers fondly believed to be 'autonomous territory' since the era of old-style 'payment by results' more than a century ago. A revised National Curriculum is promised for implementation from Autumn 2000. Its broad outlines do not suggest a curriculum fit for a new century (let alone a millennium); compared with the original National Curriculum it promises to be what this paper terms a reduced legal entitlement curriculum, more of a modification than a fundamental review. The latter is necessary in the longer term, as is a changed political climate in which primary teachers' professionalism and commitment are recognized, not undermined, and in which there is a genuine commitment on all parties to engage in the task of devising a curriculum framework for the first quarter of the twenty-first century.

The current primary curriculum has as its legal basis an act of parliament (the Education Reform Act of 1988) and associated regulations. None of the curricular requirements of that Act has been repealed, though in January 1998 it was announced that some detailed statutory requirements were to be lifted, initially at least for a limited period. While the broad framework has remained a 'given' over the last decade, the detailed regulations governing it have been subject to many modifications, especially the annual changes to assessment and reporting requirements and also, to a limited extent, modifications to content following the Dearing Review of 1993 (SCAA, 1993). *De jure* the ERA does not prescribe the totality of the primary curriculum; schools have discretion, especially since the Dearing Review, to go beyond the National Curriculum and religious education if they so wish. In the early day of its introduction there was some 'official' encouragement (from the National Curriculum Council and even from the Department of Education and Science) to make explicit provision for a range of cross-curricular issues and themes but such issues have remained minority provision (though one, citizenship, seems destined for greater prominence in future).

Neither the previous Conservative government nor the New Labour government has provided a developed rationale for the curriculum or even considered that one is desirable. The only semblance of a rationale is given in what civil servants in

1988 disparagingly called the 'motherhood and apple pie' clauses of Section 1 of the ERA which entitle every pupil in a state school to a balanced (never defined or characterized in regulations) and broadly based (never defined) curriculum which: a) promotes the spiritual, moral, cultural, mental and physical development (never defined) of the pupils at the school and of society (never clarified); and b) prepares such pupils for the opportunities, responsibilities and experiences of adult life. Recently the need for an explicit statement of the aims and purposes of the school curriculum has been recognized by the QCA (Tate, 1998) as necessary to the review of current curricular requirements. As far as the primary curriculum is concerned, given current government emphases, QCA could find no better statement from which to begin its work than the introduction to the Elementary Code of 1904 introduced as part of a liberal trend following the abolition of payment by results some years earlier (MacLure, 1986).

Even before the ERA had been passed, the government of the day had decided upon a hierarchy of subjects within the curriculum. In the 'first division' were English, mathematics and science (the latter always dangerously near to 'relegation'). As the very 'core' of the curriculum the programmes of study in these subjects were produced first, developed in most detail and made subject to national assessment arrangements. In the 'second division' were the subjects of history, geography, technology and religious education, not subject to detailed content requirements or to national assessment. Established last of all and given the most sketchy treatment in content and assessment terms were the 'third division' subjects of art, music and physical education.

Earlier this year, given the recurrent 'moral panic' over standards in numeracy and literacy, the government has reorganized its curricular hierarchy into a 'premier division' consisting only of English and mathematics (with an emphasis on reading, writing and number) and a reconstituted 'first' division of science, information technology and religious education. In these divisions the current detailed requirements in the programmes of study are still mandatory on all state primary schools. All other National Curriculum subjects have been relegated into the lowest division where the detailed (as opposed to a token) entitlement of the National Curriculum need not apply — unless primary schools choose to provide it.

As yet, in line with ERA, the government does not mandate teaching texts or materials (though those developed by the National Literacy and Numeracy Projects are likely to acquire canonical status), nor the way the curriculum is to be organized (though schools have to provide dedicated, clearly identified times each day for literacy and numeracy), nor the teaching methods to be used (though those described as 'in line with proven best practice', (DfEE, 1997b), and incorporated in government-sponsored INSET and learning materials for numeracy and literacy are being pushed very hard indeed as a new pedagogic orthodoxy).

Integral to the current National Curriculum and the government's national targets for literacy and numeracy are the legally prescribed assessment arrangements related to children's performance, currently focusing on the original core subjects (but with ICT likely to be added before too long?). These arrangements were originally designed to serve a variety of purposes simultaneously — formative, summative, evaluative and informative. In reality, however, government policy based on the recommendations of the TGAT report (DES, 1988) proved to be far ahead of the assessment 'technology' available to deliver it. As a consequence the summative aspects of individual pupil assessment are now pre-eminent along with the use of national test data to compare the performance and effectiveness of apparently 'similar' schools. That same disjuncture between policy and assessment technology continues to this day, with the current government failing to recognize the severe limitations of the testing regime on which it is relying to 'benchmark' schools and measure progress towards the achievement of its national targets. Despite the confident claims of *Excellence in Schools* (DfEE, 1997) it is *far* from certain that 'We now have sound, consistent, national measures of pupil achievement for each school at each Key Stage of the National Curriculum' (p. 25).

What effect has the National Curriculum had on practice? Certainly, the reality of the 1990s has not matched the political rhetoric of the late 1980s; nor is it likely that the reality of the very late 1990s will match current political rhetoric. Policy and practice in primary education are inevitably loose-coupled. Evidence from research and inspection tally in certain respects. It is clear from both sources that after a certain amount of initial disbelief and passive resistance primary schools have made determined efforts to implement National Curriculum requirements. Full compliance, particularly before the Dearing Review and to a lesser degree after it, has proved problematic because of content overload, and only a minority of schools have felt able to go beyond legal requirements (Galton and Fogelman, 1997). Tellingly, after a 20-year period of curriculum development prior to the passing of the ERA, those provisions of the Act which enable schools to disapply certain aspects of the National Curriculum in order to carry out educational experiments have remained inoperative as far as primary education has been concerned.

Research, inspection and monitoring by national agencies have also demonstrated very clear weaknesses in policy formulation: content overload, especially though not only in the period 1989–93; impossibly complex assessment requirements in the early stages giving rise to simplistic and flawed ones later; considerable incoherence and lack of clarity in many of the initial statutory orders; and lack of encouragement for local experimentation and discretion.

Beyond that the research evidence is equivocal. The PACE project (Pollard et al., 1994) provides evidence of change, whilst that reported by Alexander et al. (1995), Campbell and Neil (1994a, 1994b), Campbell (1997) and Plewis and Veltman (1996) suggest general continuity with previous practice rather than substantial change.

Based on my reading of HMI inspection findings prior to 1988 and of HMI/ OFSTED findings thereafter, the National Curriculum appears to have brought about real though, in political terms, unspectacular 'improvement' — at least in terms of my educational values. Overall, compared with the kind of 'curriculum lottery' (Richards, 1997a) which operated prior to 1988 there has been a more consistent curriculum entitlement offered children in English primary schools. Both whole school and individual teachers' planning has improved. Teachers have acquired a more sophisticated view of what constitutes progression and standards in the subjects they have to teach. Established curricular and pedagogic practices have been questioned and, in many schools, partially reconstituted. In Key Stage 2 in particular there has been a substantial shift towards more subject-based work, though a mixed economy of separate subject and topic work still operates in many schools, with topics becoming increasingly 'subject-focused' (i.e. concentrating on one subject and drawing on only a limited number of others where these are directly relevant) or 'subject-specific' (modules involving content and activities related to only one programme of study). Despite many initial reservations most schools have established a *modus vivendi* in relation to the subject basis of the National Curriculum. There has been a marked increase in the incidence of whole class teaching (Galton, 1998), though not to the exclusion of other forms of pupil grouping.

In general, primary-aged children have a broader curriculum than hitherto, broader both in terms of the subjects learnt and the range of content and activities within each subject. There is better continuity and progression in their learning, though passage across Key Stage interfaces continues to have an adverse effect. Children's attainment is assessed rather more accurately, especially in Key Stage 1. Pupils' standards of attainment in subjects such as science, geography and history have improved. There is no reasonably definitive evidence that in the decade since 1988 pupils' achievements in reading and number have fallen. What limited National Curriculum test data we have (and it *is* subject to all sorts of limitations) is consistent with a gradual recent rise in standards.

Up to the Secretary of State's announcement in January 1998, English primary schools have provided one of three alternative curricula:

1. Many, probably the majority, have 'played safe' and have provided a *legal entitlement curriculum* (Richards, 1997b) — teaching their pupils what the ERA required (the National Curriculum and locally determined religious education) but nothing beyond that, i.e. not attempting to create a distinctive curriculum of their own by adding other elements. Published OFSTED inspection reports provide plentiful evidence of such curricula. To use a sartorial analogy, such schools have offered 'off-the-peg curricula'.

2. Some have provided an *enriched legal entitlement curriculum,* giving their pupils their legal entitlement in terms of National Curriculum subjects and religious education but going beyond these to offer other elements to enrich the basic curriculum 'fare' in line with their particular interests, expertise or environment. Some schools, for example, have introduced 'new' subjects such as a modern foreign language or philosophy for children in one or more year groups. Some have developed 'specialist' emphases to their curricula by offering one or more subjects to a greater depth and/or range than the National Curriculum requires. Some have devoted time to teaching cross-curricular issues such as environmental education, health education or citizenship. Some have introduced programmes of personal and social development throughout the school. The more adventurous have undertaken a combination of these. To use the

sartorial analogy again, such schools have provided 'tailor-made' or 'bespoke' curricula.

3. In the light of ever-increasingly accountability demands, accusations of declining standards in the 'basics', unfavourable and ill-founded comparisons with other countries (see Galton and Morris, 1998), and an OFSTED-led curriculum focusing ever more tightly on the three original core subjects, a growing number of primary schools have provided a *neo-elementary curriculum*. These schools devote more time than ever to reading, writing and number (especially those elements found in the national tests) and giving only rudimentary, superficial 'regard' to other National Curriculum subjects. This is a curriculum similar in its broad emphases and its narrow coverage to the elementary school curriculum of the late-Victorian period. With that comparison in mind, this kind of provision might be dubbed a 'hand-me-down curriculum'.

Harder Times? The Primary Curriculum 1998–2000

What of the future of the primary curriculum? In the short-term, this *will* be determined by schools' reactions to the Secretary of State's announcement about the lifting of statutory requirements for certain subjects. In the medium-term, it *should* be influenced by the QCA's review of current curricular arrangements, though that review's conclusions could well, in retrospect, be seen to have been pre-empted by the government's move early in 1998. In the long-term, neither the Blunkett announcement nor the QCA review seems likely to lead to the fundamental reappraisal which is necessary for the early years of the new millennium.

In his letter of 13 January 1998 addressed to all primary headteachers, David Blunkett (1998) announced that:

> in advance of the Qualification and Curriculum Authority's review of the National Curriculum for the year 2000, I have decided to focus the curriculum at key stages 1 and 2 on five core subjects of English, Mathematics, Science, IT and RE. I have taken this decision so that primary schools have more time to deliver the challenging but essential literacy and numeracy targets I have set for 2002. . . . In response to concerns about the primary curriculum, I have decided to lift the statutory requirement for schools to follow the key stage 1 and 2 programmes of study in the non-core subjects of design and technology, history, geography, music, art and physical education for two years from September 1998 until a revised National Curriculum is brought in from September 2000. You will still be required to provide a broad and balanced (*sic*) curriculum.

In a parallel letter issued simultaneously Bill Stubbs, the Chairman of the QCA, reiterated that this did not mean that primary schools could focus exclusively on the five new core subjects and went on to stress that schools are required to 'have regard' to the programmes of study in the remainder (Stubbs, 1998). Guidance as to what that 'regard' may entail has been provided by the QCA, though in reality OFSTED inspectors seem likely to be the final arbiters of what it constitutes as they monitor compliance with the Secretary of State's pronouncement as part of the inspection process.

In the light of the typology offered in the previous section primary schools are likely to adopt one of five possible alternative curricula:

1. an *enriched full legal entitlement curriculum*: a theoretical option but one unlikely to be taken up given the difficulties all primary schools have found in 'fitting in' every single element of the existing statutory orders and the 'felt' pressures of individually negotiated literacy and numeracy targets;

2. an *enriched reduced legal entitlement curriculum*: a more likely choice than 1 for those schools wanting to provide their own distinctive curricula, attracted by the opportunity of leaving out problematic elements of some programmes of study but also aware of the need to find more time beyond the literacy and numeracy hours to implement the full programmes of study in English and mathematics;

3. a *full legal entitlement curriculum*: a possible but not a frequent choice given the difficulties of providing adequate coverage of every element of all the programmes of study and the pressures resulting from target setting;

4. a *reduced legal entitlement curriculum*: a likely choice for those schools taking notions of curricular breadth and balance seriously but wanting to take some advantage of the opportunity to 'cut curricular corners' and find some more time for mathematics and English outside the dedicated literacy and numeracy hours;

5. a *neo-elementary curriculum*: in line with their pre-1998 curriculum in the case of some schools, and a conscious choice by others feeling particularly pressurized by factors such as OFSTED re-inspections; being in 'special measures'; having 'serious weaknesses'; performing less well than their 'benchmark' counterparts; or generally suffering from 'overstrain'.

There is a very real likelihood that many schools, not just those in Education Action Zones, will opt out of the entitlement curriculum and provide a *neo-elementary curriculum*, not necessarily out of conviction (though some will hold such values) but out of a feeling of constraint and coercion. If so, many of the improvements accruing from the introduction of the National Curriculum will be put at risk or even nullified.

References

ALEXANDER, R., WILLCOCK, J. and NELSON, N. (1995) 'Change and continuity', in ALEXANDER, R. (ed.) *Versions of Primary Education*, London: Routledge.

BLUNKETT, D. (1998) Letter to all headteachers of Key Stage 1 and Key Stage 2 schools in England, 13 January.

CAMPBELL, R. (1997) *Standards of Literacy and Numeracy in Primary Schools: A Real or Manufactured Crisis?* Occasional paper, CREPE, University of Warwick.

CAMPBELL, R. and NEIL, S. (1994a) *Primary Teachers at Work*, London: Routledge.

CAMPBELL, R. and NEIL, S. (1994b) *Curriculum Reform at Key Stage 1: Teacher Commitment and Policy Failure*, London: Longman.

DEARING, R. (1993) *The National Curriculum and Assessment: Final Report*, London: School Curriculum and Assessment Authority.

DEPARTMENT OF EDUCATION AND SCIENCE (DES) (1988) *National Curriculum Task Group on Assessment and Testing: A Report*, London: Department of Education and Science.

DEPARTMENT FOR EDUCATION AND EMPLOYMENT (DfEE) (1997) *Excellence in Schools*, London: Her Majesty's Stationery Office.

GALTON, M. (1998) *Reliving the ORACLE Experience: Back to Basics or Back to the Future?* Occasional paper, CREPE, University of Warwick.

GALTON, M. and FOGELMAN, K. (1997) *The Use of Discretionary Time in the Primary School*, Final report of research commissioned by the National Union of Teachers, University of Leicester School of Education.

GALTON, M. and MORRIS, P. (1998) 'The real lessons from the Pacific Rim', *Education 3–13*, **26**, 2.

MacLURE, S. (1986) *Educational Documents: England and Wales 1816 to the Present Day*, London: Methuen.

PLEWIS, I. and VELTMAN, M. (1996) 'Where does all the time go? Changes in pupils' experience in Year 2 classrooms', in HUGHES, M. (ed.) *Teaching and Learning in Changing Times*, Oxford: Blackwell.

POLLARD, A. et al. (1994) *Changing English Primary Schools?*, London: Cassell.

RICHARDS, C. (1997a) 'Enrichment as entitlement', *Developing the Primary School Curriculum: The Next Steps*, London: School Curriculum and Assessment Authority.

RICHARDS, C. (1997b) 'The primary curriculum 1988–2008', *British Journal of Curriculum and Assessment*, **7**, 3.

RICHARDS, C. (1998) 'Curriculum and pedagogy in Key Stage 2: A survey of policy and practice in small rural primary schools', *The Curriculum Journal*, **9**, 3.

STUBBS, W. (1998) Letter to all headteachers of Key Stage 1 and Key Stage 2 schools in England, 13 January.

Part 3

Primary Pedagogy

12   Teaching Methods: Some Distinctions

It has become commonplace to suggest that immediately after the Education Reform Act of 1988 the 'what' of education took precedence over the 'how' and that in more recent years the reverse had been the case. That may have been so for policy-makers and their advisers at national level but was not so for primary practitioners for whom curriculum and teaching methods were inextricably linked from the outset. It is true that with the publication of Curriculum Organisation and Classroom Practice in Primary Schools (DES, 1992) and further initiatives from OFSTED and, more recently, from the Standards and Effectiveness Unit (SEU) of the DfEE, discussion and prescription about pedagogy have become more prominent. Yet debate has been conducted along very simplistic lines. Much of it has been concerned with the merits of whole class, individual and group teaching, as if these were clearly defined teaching methods, which they are not, and with a limited range of teaching techniques (instruction, exposition, questioning) as if these constituted an adequate pedagogic repertoire, which they do not. This chapter attempts to provide much needed clarification.

The National Curriculum as established by the Education Reform Act has three major components:

i)   attainment targets which relate to the 'knowledge, skills and understanding' which pupils are to acquire;
ii) programmes of study which relate to 'the matters, skills and processes' to be taught;
iii) assessment arrangements.

The National Curriculum does not prescribe how the school curriculum should be organized, nor does it prescribe the teaching methods to be used to cover the programmes of study in the required range and depth. In fact, the Education Reform Act explicitly rules out the Secretary of State requiring particular teaching methods and forms of organization. They are to be left as matters for professional choice and judgment.

Grouping

In teaching primary school children, teachers have to make decisions about the *methods* to use to help children learn and about the *grouping* arrangements to employ. Too often discussion in primary education does not distinguish clearly enough between these two kinds of decisions. Grouping is an aspect of organization and should not be confused with teaching methods. For example, while the teacher may organize work for individuals, for small groups or for the whole class, the method of teaching she employs might be the same in each case. Under each of those organizational arrangements, she might choose to explain, or give information, or set the children off on an enquiry or require them to read for information, or adopt any combination of those and other teaching processes. Equally, while another teacher might concentrate on teaching the whole class together rather than teaching groups or individuals, she is likely to use a wide variety of teaching methods.

Grouping is but a means to an end — the effective promotion of children's learning. Any form of grouping (be it whole class, small group or individual) should be employed where it appears to 'work', where it is a reasonably effective but efficient way of organizing pupils to secure their learning. There is no self-evident way of organizing pupils to secure their learning. There is no self-evident virtue in individual work, in group work or in whole class work unless the form of grouping fosters, rather than hinders, the realization of the teacher's learning objectives. We need to acknowledge that for some purposes whole class teaching might be appropriate for primary-aged children, while accepting that on occasion children should work in groups, just as they should spend time in independent study. What is required is a mixed economy where different forms of pupil grouping are adopted for different pedagogic purposes.

Teaching Methods

The OFSTED discussion paper, *Primary Matters* reports a strong association between the quality of teaching and the standards achieved. It draws attention to a number of aspects of pedagogy — in particular, the teacher's ability to use questions effectively to assess pupils' knowledge and to challenge their thinking, and the teacher's effective use of exposition and instruction. It does *not* argue that only these are important; it does argue that they are all essential components in any primary teacher's pedagogic repertoire.

Under the broad heading of teaching methods it may be helpful to distinguish three aspects: *teaching techniques, teaching media*, and *teaching objectives*. All three aspects are involved in any act of teaching.

Teachers use *teaching techniques* when they engage in one or more of the following activities intended to bring about pupils' learning:

- instructing
- describing
- clarifying
- explaining

- recalling
- demonstrating
- questioning
- prompting
- interpreting
- illustrating
- evaluating
- predicting
- eliciting
- speculating
- previewing
- reviewing.

The list is not exhaustive; teachers use other techniques to foster pupils' learning. Some techniques are *direct* — involving the transmission of knowledge, understanding and skills, e.g. instruction, demonstration, explanation. Others are *indirect* — involving degrees of pupil interpretation and participation, e.g. questioning, prompting, eliciting pupils' ideas, supporting children's enquiries, etc. Often several techniques are employed in the same lesson or session.

Every act of teaching also involves the use of a *medium* or *media*: most often teacher talk, or 'surrogate' teacher talk if tasks are set or children instructed through written means such as workcards or worksheets. Other media include broadcasts, books, blackboards, computer programs, visits, handling materials of different kinds, and other first-hand experience. Many lessons involve the use of more than one medium.

In employing particular techniques and media, teachers have implicit or explicit *purposes* in mind. They intend that in relation to the content being taught or learned in the lesson or session, pupils should engage in one or more of the activities listed under teaching techniques: i.e. pupils might be expected to record information, describe phenomena, explain processes, demonstrate skills, offer interpretations or engage in speculation, etc. Some teaching purposes may be *closed* in the sense that the pupils are expected to respond in predictable ways and with predictable outcomes: e.g. they might have to emulate directly the skills taught by the teacher; they might have to repeat the teacher's explanation more or less in his or her own words; they might have to write down the teacher's descriptions of events or phenomena. Some teaching purposes may be more *open*: the pupils might be expected, for example, to describe or interpret, but in their own words and in their own terms; they might have to illustrate aspects of the content being taught but may be able to represent this content in more than one way. Some teaching purposes may be *open* — deliberately encouraging a diversity of response and interpretation so, for example, the children might be encouraged to offer their own speculations about events in the past; or to offer their own questions for further investigation; or to evaluate using their own criteria. Thus, depending on the teacher's purposes, teaching might involve transmission *to* pupils, transaction *with* pupils, personal interpretation or initiative *by* pupils, or a combination of these.

Too often teaching methods are still discussed, not in terms of the wide range of techniques, media and purposes outlined above, but in terms of broad, vague categories, often in contrasting pairs: 'formal' versus 'informal' methods; 'traditional' versus 'progressive' processes; or 'exploratory' versus 'didactic' teaching. Such crude opposites do not do justice to the wide range of teaching techniques and media needed to foster children's learning in and beyond the National Curriculum.

Too often, also, teaching techniques have been criticized or supported without reference to the kinds of learning they are intended to foster: for example, instructing children has been seen as undesirable irrespective of the context; demonstration by the teacher in art or physical education has been viewed as stifling children's creativity; closed questions have been attacked for encouraging uncritical recall. Likewise, but from different quarters, providing children with opportunities to devise and conduct their own fair tests has been viewed by some as irrelevant; or encouraging them to explain things for themselves has been seen as less important than their being able to recite the teacher's explanation.

Although very general and in need of 'unpacking' in particular contexts, the criterion which teachers need to use when choosing teaching media and techniques is that of 'fitness for purpose', i.e. do the teaching media and techniques foster the kind of learning required in that context with that child or those children? Different contexts (including differences among children) involve different learning requirements; different learning requirements necessitate different techniques or media. In the light of the National Curriculum many, though by no means all, of its knowledge, skills and understanding requirements are likely to be met through the employment of a range of direct teaching techniques to fulfil relatively closed teaching purposes. However, for some aspects of the programmes of study, indirect teaching methods are needed. The repertoire of teaching techniques and media available to teachers is wide but fitness for purpose should govern the judgments they make.

In order to choose appropriate techniques primary teachers need four kinds of knowledge and understanding: i) they need to understand, and to have experience of, the strengths and weaknesses associated with a wide range of techniques; ii) they need to know which techniques are likely to be required for different children; iii) they need to be aware of National Curriculum requirements; iv) and they need to know what constitutes progression in the subjects they are required to teach. Very many primary teachers possess the first three of these; many need to develop deeper subject knowledge and adjust their teaching techniques accordingly.

In summary, it is important to acknowledge the complexity of teaching involving, as it does, professional judgment about the appropriate 'mix' of techniques, media and purposes in any teaching situation. The 'educational engagement' can only be, has to be, fostered in a variety of different ways.

Reference

OFFICE FOR STANDARDS IN EDUCATION (1994) *Primary Matters*, London: OFSTED.

13 'The Three Wise Men's Report': A Critical Appraisal

The Education Reform Act of 1988 did not prescribe the organization of the curric-
ulum, the materials to be used or the teaching approaches to be employed. It is
unclear how far this was due to political sensitivities over possible opposition to such
moves which could prejudice the implementation of the National Curriculum; how
far to a genuine wish to preserve teacher autonomy in this area; or how far to
a realization that in the final analysis it is impossible to prescribe in detail how
individual teachers will operate in the privacy of their own classrooms.

However, some three years later, with a general election in the offing the then
Secretary of State, Kenneth Clarke, and his acolytes began increasingly to intervene
both in the actual content of the National Curriculum and in relation to pedagogy
through their attacks on 'child-centred' education which they considered to be
hindering the effective 'delivery' of the curriculum in primary schools. As part of this
political offensive they commissioned a paper 'to review available evidence about
the delivery of education in primary schools' and to make recommendations. The
result was the publication early in 1992 of Curriculum Organisation and Classroom
Practice in Primary Schools, *otherwise known as the 'Three Wise Men's Report'.*
This was widely interpreted as an attack on primary schools by their detractors and
as a defence of primary schools by their supporters. It was selectively quoted and
misquoted in subsequent debate. Contrary to what was commonly believed it did
not present any definitive conclusions: it was intended to stimulate, rather than
foreclose, discussion, and in many ways it was reasonably successful in this
regard. Nevertheless, it had considerable weaknesses, as this review, written in
1992, attempts to point out. In particular its terms of reference side-stepped the key
issue of the time — the much needed reconstitution of the National Curriculum — an
issue which soon demanded governmental and professional attention and which
diverted some of the energies generated by the production of the 1992 document.

The paper, *Curriculum Organisation and Classroom Practice in Primary Schools*,
was written in response to the Secretary of State's request 'to review available
evidence about the delivery of education in primary schools' and 'make recommendations about curriculum organisation, teaching methods and classroom practice
appropriate for the successful implementation of the National Curriculum, particularly at Key Stage 2'. There are several important points to note: the paper was
intended to review evidence but not to provide new evidence of its own; it was to
make recommendations rather than reach definitive or authoritative conclusions; it

was to focus on organization and methodology, not on curriculum content; it was to be written to help in the successful implementation of the National Curriculum, especially *at Key Stage 2*.

I believe the paper succeeds admirably in meeting its brief, though I believe its brief to be importantly flawed. In consequence, the paper's relevance to the key problem facing primary education is currently partial rather than very substantial. The paper is an important, almost (but not quite) timely document. Its status needs to be stressed: it is a *discussion* paper, not a report, written by three individuals, two of whom have extensive experience of primary education (though only one of these in primary schools). Its concerns — pedagogy and organization — are at the very heart of primary teachers' professionalism; it touches many sensitive issues (for the most sensitively); it is intended to foster a much needed but difficult professional debate.

The paper is clear, straightforward and logical — in sharp (and, in some ways, inappropriate) contrast to the messy, often only partially rational, world of class-room life it addresses. It has some powerful insights into the difficulties facing teachers (for example, in relation to differentiation) but is not as sympathetic as it might be to the problem of schools and teachers struggling to cope with multiple innovations introduced all too quickly. It valuably summarizes the evidence from classroom research but treats it uncritically, imbues it with an authority it does not possess and suggests a concurrence in its conclusions which I find unwarranted. I share the paper's concern about educational standards, especially whether current standards constitute an adequate preparation for the demands of life in modern society, but I believe the paper makes too much of shaky evidence 'of downward trends in important aspects of literacy and numeracy'. A chapter on 'Standards of Achievement in Primary Schools' is undoubtedly necessary, but I believe ought to have been merely one sentence long: 'There is insufficient evidence to settle the question of whether standards generally, or in numeracy and literacy in particular, have risen or fallen in recent years.' It is far from clear, anyway, what would con-stitute adequate evidence to settle such a complex, value-laden, and emotive issue.

I have already stated that the remit given by the Secretary of State was flawed but have not indicated why. It was flawed because it assumed the continuance of the National Curriculum in its current form and asked for the issues of curriculum organization and classroom practice to be addressed on that assumption. This, the authors of the paper do. In doing so, I believe they inevitably fail to address the major problem facing primary schools and offer recommendations which, even if adopted in their entirety, would not do much to ease the pressures or reduce the predicaments facing the staffs of primary schools. The key issue facing schools at present (and in the next two to five years) is the manageability of the National Curriculum; the paper sidesteps rather than addresses the issue.

The paper is at its strongest when discussing organizational strategies and teaching techniques. It valuably distinguishes between teaching methods or tech-niques which teachers use to help children learn and the grouping or organizational strategies they employ; too often in the past the two have been confused. The section on whole class, group and individual teaching is particularly detailed and well argued; it repays much careful attention and thought. There can be little doubt that teachers need the skill and the judgment to be able to select and apply whatever grouping strategies are appropriate to the task in hand. Many more teachers than the paper implies or acknowledges already possess such skills and exercise such judgment. The paper is right, too, to reinstate the importance of whole class teaching though it draws on its strengths rather than its weaknesses. There is no doubt, however, that in skilled hands whole class teaching can enhance pupils' involvement and judgment while in unskilled hands it can unduly restrict them.

The paper appropriately emphasizes the importance of teaching techniques, such as explaining, questioning and instructing and the need to create opportunities for these techniques to be used purposefully. It ought, too, to have emphasized the importance of other direct methods — as when face to face with children teachers describe, demonstrate, interpret, define, predict or speculate. All of these need a place in each teacher's pedagogic armoury. Disappointingly the paper has little to say about the importance of *indirect* teaching methods where, through the use of media such as computer programs, broadcasts, worksheets, books, first-hand experience or talk, teachers provide opportunities for children themselves to explain, question, instruct, describe, define, predict, etc. As the paper itself acknowledges, fitness for purpose should govern choice of teaching techniques. Many, though by no means all, of the National Curriculum's knowledge, skills and understanding requirements can be appropriately met through the employment of direct teaching methods; however, there will be an important and, for some attainment targets, indispensable place for indirect methods. The paper should acknowledge this.

The section on strengthening curriculum expertise makes many valuable points: in particular, the need for a dispassionate examination of the most sacred of 'sacred cows', the class teacher system; the need for greater subject expertise if teachers are to manage and transact work related to National Curriculum programmes of study; and the need to revise urgently LEA's LMS formulae in favour of primary schools. The paper's analysis of four broad teaching roles (the generalist, generalist/consultant, semi-specialist and specialist) is analytically sound. Its recommendation that each school should work out its particular combination of teaching roles has to be right in theory but fails to take account of funding (and therefore staffing) realities in primary schools as they currently operate and are likely to operate in the foreseeable future. In all but the very largest primary schools, it would be impossible to employ full-time specialist teachers for more than one or two National Curriculum subjects and in most primary schools developing a reasonable measure of semi-specialization (except teacher exchange of classes) would be difficult without more staffing 'slack' in the system. No other developed country staffs its primary or elementary schools to enable subject specialization to occur except in a subsidiary way; in Japan, for example, music and art are the only subjects where considerable specialist teaching occurs and then not fully in every school.

Realistically, the class teacher system is likely to remain the dominant mode — certainly in Key Stage 1, and almost certainly in Years 3 and 4 in Key Stage 2. In Years 5 and 6, the class teacher role is unlikely to disappear altogether; there will still be the need for one teacher to be responsible for ensuring that a particular class receives a curriculum adequate in range and depth, even if that teacher does not teach the whole of that class's timetable him or herself. The issue facing primary schools in the foreseeable future is how to use specialist expertise to provide the necessary support to generalist teachers. A spectrum of support is needed which takes a variety of forms depending on the individual and the subject in question: occasional advice from a teacher with specialist knowledge; a detailed scheme of work; reading books or distance learning materials to enhance subject knowledge; attendance at INSET run by an outside agency or provided by the school itself; cooperative teaching with one or more colleagues; a coordinator working alongside the individual teacher for a time to introduce new aspects of work; a teacher with specialist knowledge taking a particular aspect of a programme of study for a limited period; or a teacher with specialist knowledge taking over the teaching of a particular subject for the whole year.

Such support should be made available, circumstances permitting, to all members of staff whether they teach Key Stage 1 or Key Stage 2 classes; the last two forms of support are more likely to be needed by teachers in Years 5 and 6. To provide this support, schools need to engage in flexible, sensitive patterns of staff deployment — far more complex than traditional secondary patterns. Such modes of staff deployment will need to shift over time and be responsive to changing circumstances; such circumstances would vary from term to term or even within a term, not just on a yearly basis. This presents a very challenging task for primary headteachers.

Timing

I began by stating that the paper is an important, almost timely, document. My major concern is that its publication may deflect the teaching profession from debating the more important issue of how the National Curriculum might be reconstituted so as to preserve its undoubted benefits but to ease its impossible raft of demands. Once the outline of a reconstituted National Curriculum becomes apparent, then the important and long overdue debate on curriculum organization and classroom practice should begin. I believe, and this is very much to the credit of the authors of the paper, that such a debate would result in many of their recommendations being accepted — many, but not *all*.

14 Whole Class Teaching: A Reappraisal

There is no doubt that following the publication of the Plowden Report in 1967, the end of selection in most local education authorities and the widespread adoption of mixed ability, often mixed-age, classes, most primary school teachers in the 1970s had to reappraise the way they organized the teaching of their children. In particular, there was widespread use of more individualized approaches, complemented in some classes by more systematic use of group work. In the vast majority of classes, teachers continued to teach the whole class for some subjects such as music or physical education, but also for aspects of work such as 'creative writing' or storytime in English. There was not the wholesale abandonment of that method of grouping that its more recent advocates have implied. However, it is probably true to say that whole class teaching (WCT) did not receive as much emphasis as in the pre-Plowden period, and that in the 1970s and 1980s excessively complicated forms of organization and grouping developed, along with undue reliance on individualized teaching approaches, in a significant but unknown proportion of primary classrooms.

Criticisms of such forms of organization are not new. As far back as 1977, when reflecting on the implications of Neville Bennett's (1976) research reported in Teaching Styles and Pupil Progress, I argued that:

> it should make us think very carefully about the forms of classroom organisation we employ. It could well be that some forms of classroom organisation are dysfunctional: they are so time- and energy-consuming simply to maintain that teachers are unable to devote themselves to their major task: seeing that children are learning worthwhile things and acquiring worthwhile attitudes to learning . . . In particular we need to think hard about 'individualised learning', especially where this involves children working daily through a programme of work cards, work sheets and so on — supposedly at their own pace but in reality at a pace determined by the speed and success of the hard-pressed teacher in monitoring such work . . . Does this form of organisation leave much room for teaching as opposed to management? . . . Does it provide children with the necessary stimulus for question-posing and problem-solving? Do children get enough exposure to the richness and flexibility of adult language which can help them acquire concepts and understand explanations? I have my doubts on all these points. . . . If nothing else, Bennett's research suggests that no one form of organisation is equally effective with all children, *a fairly obvious point but one whose implications are not always worked through in practice.* There is a place for individualised learning, but also a place for the shared experience of class teaching. In particular, I would argue we need to give far greater attention to small-group teaching than we do. *This is much neglected but, I believe, does make much more economical and fruitful use of teachers' scarce expertise, time and, especially, language, than does over-reliance on other modes. (Education 3–13, 5, 2, 1977; emphasis added in 1999)*

That still remains my position over 20 years later. Teaching the whole class is a reasonably efficient and effective way of organizing pupils in order to teach many, though by no means all, the requirements of the National Curriculum. But the neglected art of small group teaching needs to be given a much greater focus of attention in professional development. In my judgment, probably one of the most beneficial aspects of the national literacy and numeracy strategies may be the stimulus they give to systematic, daily, small group teaching, not the prominence they accord to whole class teaching.

But of course, whole class teaching does have its advantages as well as its drawbacks. This chapter, written in 1996, attempts to provide a balanced appraisal of this form of pupil grouping (not teaching method) and to indicate the kinds of contexts in which it may profitably be used.

What Is Whole Class Teaching?

Teaching can involve a teacher working with individuals, pairs of pupils, groups or the entire class; it can employ a wide variety of techniques such as explanation, demonstration, illustration, speculation and questioning; it can take place in a variety of contexts — classroom, hall, playing field, etc. Whole class teaching (WCT) involves all members of a class being engaged simultaneously in interaction with the teacher; it does not assume any particular set of teaching techniques or any particular context. It is essentially an organizational or grouping strategy.

Since the establishment of elementary education in the nineteenth century, WCT has played a very important part in transacting the curriculum in those schools large enough to form separate classes of pupils for teaching purposes. During the last 30 years or so, it has been complemented (and in many schools largely supplanted) by other forms of grouping such as individual and/or group work. In other European states and in the countries of the Pacific Rim such as Japan, Taiwan and Korea it remains the dominant grouping strategy for all or almost all subjects.

Why the Interest in Whole Class Teaching?

Recently in England there has been renewed interest in exploring the potential of WCT in primary schools. International studies of primary pupils' achievements have raised issues about the effectiveness of current grouping practices and teaching techniques; the difficulties teachers have faced in implementing the National Curriculum have promoted questioning about both the 'what' of the curriculum and the 'how' of teaching; evidence from HMI has pointed to the 'stubborn' continuance of a significant proportion of unsatisfactory teaching. The DES discussion paper of 1992, *Curriculum Organisation and Classroom Practice in Primary Schools*, has reviewed classroom research and other evidence and has argued for the need to re-examine the place of WCT, and, in particular, the need to use grouping practices and teaching techniques which are 'fit for purpose'. Subsequent OFSTED discussion papers, HMCI's Annual Lecture of 1995 and the OFSTED paper *Teaching Quality*, have focused attention on primary pedagogy and in particular the part to be played by WCT.

How Can Whole Class Teaching Be Used?

WCT can be used for all or part of a lesson or session. Reading an extract from a children's novel may be followed by class discussion; listening to a poem may lead to an exploration of the meanings the poet is attempting to convey; listening to a song may lead to its learning by the whole class. In each of these cases, the entire class may be corporately, and positively, engaged in the same activity for the whole of the lesson.

In different circumstances, the demonstration and explanation of an experiment given by a teacher to all pupils may be followed for part of the time by work in which small groups of pupils carry out similar, though not necessarily identical, experiments. Ideas and activities in dance suggested by the teacher to the whole class may be followed up by individual or small group work in which sequences of ideas and activities are put together. Mental mathematics involving quick-fire questions on number bonds involving all the children but pitched at different levels for different pupils may be followed by individual work on number operations for the remainder of the lesson. Whole class teaching may quite appropriately take up a varying proportion of a lesson or session depending on the purposes the teacher has in mind.

WCT can play a valuable part in the teaching of all subjects, though the extent of its usefulness will vary according to the aspects of the programmes of study being taught. For example, it can be an efficient and effective way of transmitting content knowledge of materials or living things in science; it can help pupils understand why individuals such as Henry VIII or societies such as the Romans acted as they did; it can give children background information to help them appreciate why particular pieces of music or other works of art were produced.

However, WCT cannot give pupils experience of devising their own 'fair tests' in science; or comparing historical resources to provide their own interpretation of events; or composing pieces of music or expressing their own ideas in paint. It can, however, provide general guidance and underlying principles to help individuals or groups work more efficiently and effectively on such activities.

What Are the Advantages and Disadvantages of Whole Class Teaching?

Compared with group or individual work WCT provides a greater (though never total) degree of control for teachers over the teaching and learning taking place in their classrooms. With WCT teachers not only determine the kind of work to be undertaken by their pupils (as they do with individual or group work) but they also have more direct, personal control of how that work is done. The structure, rhythm and methodology of the lesson are theirs to determine closely and, very importantly, theirs to alter in the light of changing circumstances as the lesson unfolds. That control is not necessarily heavy handed or constraining; exercised sensitively it can enhance the quality of learning by helping ensure that teachers' objectives for lessons are met or by allowing for the exploration of unexpected issues when teachers judge them to be educationally worthwhile. Teachers can exercise these degrees of control and discretion more easily in class lessons than in situations where three, four or more groups are simultaneously engaged in different activities or when large numbers of individual pupils are pursuing their own enquiries.

WCT is more likely to result in lessons with a clear, recognizable structure. Teachers can focus on a limited number of ideas, pieces of information or skills to be conveyed; can introduce lessons by reference to past related work; can spend time developing the focus of the lesson; can set work to foster pupils' understanding of ideas or application of skills; and, very importantly, can 'draw together the threads' towards the end of lessons to review what has been taught and learnt and to point the way forward to future work. The basic structure of whole class lessons — introduction, development, consolidation and review — lends itself to a wide variety of interpretations of varying degrees of sophistication depending on teachers' skills, the content to be taught and the pupils' responses. The same structure can be applied also to group work, though it requires considerable skill on teachers' part to ensure that they pay sufficient time and attention to each phase of a group's work in the light of the often pressing demands made by other groups simultaneously working on other activities.

Pupils' interest and involvement in their work can be stimulated in a wide variety of ways. The content of the work may appeal to them; the medium in which they are working may enthuse them; the end-product to which they are working may be motivating; but more often than not the crucial factor is the ability of teachers to create, sustain and develop interest through verbal interaction with their pupils, even though this may be complemented by the use of media such as broadcasts, pictures, computer programs or videos. The importance of teacher talk in developing motivation and involvement cannot be over-estimated. Compared with other forms of grouping, WCT maximizes the opportunities for pupils to listen to teacher talk and to engage with it through questioning and dialogue. Through WCT, teachers can concentrate on that interaction, rather than on the organization and servicing of individuals and groups, and can, in principle at least, reach all pupils simultaneously and engage their attention. While no form of teaching guarantees that all individuals will be interested or involved, evidence from classroom observational studies suggests that pupils' levels of attention and the extent of their 'on-task' behaviour are generally higher in lessons characterized by a significant proportion of whole class teaching than where individual or small group work predominates.

Perhaps the greatest advantages of WCT are that it enables teachers to focus single-mindedly on one set of objectives for the class as a whole rather than a large number of objectives related to the work of individuals or groups, and that it enables them to concentrate on the skilful employment of those teaching methods which they judge 'fit for purpose' in achieving their objectives. These methods may be many and varied. Centrally they include instruction, explanation, illustration, clarification, demonstration and different forms of questioning; in addition, teachers on occasion engage in activities such as interpretation, evaluation, prediction, speculation, previewing and reviewing.

Because of the limited focus in a class lesson, teachers have more time and opportunity to deploy such methods sensitively. For example, they can take time to explain phenomena or events in different ways if the class or part of it finds difficulty with one particular kind of explanation. They can use a range of closed or open questions; give pupils sufficient time to think and answer; and, as the lesson progresses, increase the degree of challenge in their questioning in the light of pupils' responses. Because they are less pressurized for time or by a multiplicity of demands, teachers can actively involve pupils in taking lessons forward by asking them to explain their work at some length, to develop their thinking aloud or to lead part of the lesson by, for example, working out examples at the blackboard. Teachers can take more time to 'model' advanced thinking skills such as inference, prediction or speculation, and they have more time to demonstrate alternative ways of thinking and problem solving, confident in the knowledge that groups of pupils are not unoccupied while awaiting their turn for attention.

The major disadvantage of WCT is its inability to provide differentially for the full range of abilities likely to be present in mixed ability, sometimes mixed-age, classes typically found in primary schools. However good the teacher's explanation, however skilful their questioning or employment of other teaching techniques, at least some of the content of any lesson is likely to be inappropriate or inaccessible for a sizeable proportion of the class. The content may fail to challenge or stimulate the more able pupils if, as is often the case, it is pitched at those of average or those of slightly below average ability in the subject. Equally, pitched too high, the content may result in the slower-learning pupils failing to understand aspects of the work. WCT can attempt to cater for diversity by appealing directly at various times in the lesson to pupils of differing abilities but, even so, for a proportion of the time many pupils are not likely to be able to engage fully or profitably with the content.

Such limitations also occur to some degree when teachers engage in group teaching since different members of a group, whatever its size, will have different levels of knowledge, understanding and skills. However, teachers are more likely to provide better matched material to groups of pupils than to the class as a whole. In theory, individual teaching can overcome the problem of poor match of task to ability, provided the teacher can diagnose the strengths and weaknesses of individuals and teach them accordingly. In practice, in classes of around 30 pupils catering for such individual differences is impossible in every subject or for every pupil in any one subject, though it is perhaps attainable in some aspects of work.

What Is the Place of WCT?

WCT is a reasonably efficient and reasonably effective way of organizing pupils in order to teach many, though not all, aspects of the National Curriculum. It has its limitations, especially in relation to the vexed issue of differentiation, but so do group and individual teaching. No form of grouping is a panacea; no form provides the ideal context in which teachers can employ the full range of teaching techniques required to ensure that all pupils are fully engaged in every aspect of the National Curriculum. What is required in primary classes is a 'mixed economy' where different forms of pupil grouping are adopted for different purposes — and WCT should feature prominently in every teacher's repertoire.

15 Teachers' 'Subject' Knowledge: Some Distinctions and Requirements

A great deal has been talked about the place of subject knowledge in primary education. To some, teachers' knowledge at their own level of the major concepts, principles, skills and content of established disciplines such as mathematics or science is seen as of paramount importance and as having been neglected in both preservice and inservice education. To others, that 'high level' knowledge has been seen as irrelevant to the task of teaching young children.

Discussion on the issue of subject knowledge has been bedevilled by lack of clarity rather than by a dispassionate examination of the knowledge requirements of primary school teachers. As this chapter, written in 1994, points out, there are at least three kinds of subject knowledge needed (along with other types of knowledge): subject content knowledge, subject application knowledge and curriculum knowledge.

If the issue is looked at logically, it is clear that subject content knowledge is necessary — a teacher needs to be reasonably confident that she understands, at an appropriate level, what she has to teach before she teaches it. However such necessary knowledge is not sufficient for successful teaching — knowing x does not necessarily entail knowing how to teach x. Such subject content knowledge needs to be cashed out in terms of how it can be 'translated' into terms which young children can understand, i.e. subject application knowledge. Both kinds of knowledge are necessary but not sufficient to enable teachers to meet National Curriculum requirements: curriculum knowledge is also required. And, of course, all three kinds of subject knowledge are necessary but not sufficient to ensure children's learning: other kinds of knowledge and experience — of pedagogy, child development, social interaction, knowledge of individual children, etc. — come into play. There is a great danger that particularly with the introduction of the National Curriculum for Initial Teacher Training an undue emphasis is being placed on subject content knowledge at the expense of the other knowledges required.

Changes to the National Curriculum are likely to reduce the statutory requirements made on generalist class teachers in terms of the range and volume of the work they need to undertake. The National Curriculum will, however, remain demanding — paradoxically more demanding on teachers than on pupils. Reconstituted programmes of study, however detailed, will continue to require 'subject' knowledge which some — perhaps many — primary school teachers, through no fault of their own, do not yet possess. The same will apply to newly qualified teachers whose knowledge of the non-core subjects is likely to be rudimentary given the focus of the National Curriculum for Initial Teacher Training on English, mathematics, science and ITC. Providing work that challenges high-attaining pupils, particularly but not only at the end of Key Stage 2, is far from easy in subjects where teachers feel less confident. Provided teacher assessment remains an important component of the national assessment regime it requires considerable knowledge, not only of the children themselves, but also of the subject matter they are learning.

A key issue for primary schools is to identify the subject expertise currently residing — often hidden — within their staff. Such expertise may have been the result of teachers' higher education, of their attendance at inservice courses, or of their long-term personal interests and enthusiasms. Three forms of subject expertise are needed and all three are equally important: knowledge of subject content, knowledge of how to apply subject content knowledge in teaching primary-aged children, and knowledge of National Curriculum requirements.

Subject content knowledge involves knowledge of the main concepts, principles, skills and content of particular disciplines such as mathematics or history. This is indepth knowledge at the adult's own level. Particular members of staff in a primary school are likely to have well-developed subject content knowledge but only in depth for one or two subjects of the curriculum. Possession of such content knowledge is probably more common in schools than is generally acknowledged, either by primary school teachers themselves or their detractors. Many teachers underestimate the value and depth of their subject content knowledge gained in college, or from other sources.

The second kind of subject knowledge involves the *application of subject knowledge* in teaching young children. This involves knowing how to make the knowledge, skills and understanding of a subject accessible and meaningful to children — how best to represent particular ideas; what kinds of illustrations or metaphors to use; what examples to draw on; what kinds of explanations to offer or questions to pose; how to relate what needs to be taught to children's experiences or interests, and so on. This applied expertise may develop from initial or inservice training, or from 'the wisdom of practice'. As with subject content knowledge, many teachers may not appreciate how much they know about the teaching of particular subjects or aspects of subjects. Too often such knowledge remains tacit. Sometimes for reasons of modesty, self-defensiveness or sheer possessiveness, teachers may be reluctant to share their applied expertise with colleagues. There is a good deal of 'applied wisdom' locked up in the minds, plans and practices of individual teachers that could, with profit, be more widely available within schools.

The third aspect of subject knowledge is more readily acknowledged in most schools. This is *curriculum knowledge*, i.e. knowledge of National Curriculum requirements; of national strategies and project materials; of policies, guidelines and schemes of work; and of the range of published materials and sources available as 'tools of the trade' to help teachers transact the curriculum. This constitutes the acceptable 'public face' of subject expertise in many primary schools.

Schools need to carry out an audit of the subject expertise (including all three components) of their teaching staff and create a climate in which teachers are able to develop and share their subject expertise, irrespective of whether they hold any formally designated responsibilities for the management of a subject. The headteacher's subject knowledge should be included in any appraisal of the expertise available and steps should be taken over time to match more closely subject responsibilities with the *content, applied* and *curriculum knowledge* available on the staff. Gaps in expertise should be remedied partly by the appointment of new staff (including newly qualified teachers) with specifically required subject knowledge, and partly by building expertise from the existing complement of staff.

16   Subject Expertise and Its Deployment

Over the last ten years, the primary community has had to re-examine some of its basic assumptions and practices — an exercise for which it has not received the credit it deserves. One such tradition is the generalist role of the class teacher. Twenty years ago, one of the major planks of primary teachers' claim to profes- sionalism lay in their supposed ability, single-handedly and without any help from other colleagues, to teach the whole of the curriculum to their classes throughout the school year. However, with the advent of the National Curriculum, that claim became untenable. Teachers, some reluctantly, began to acknowledge that it was virtually impossible to teach unaided the full range of the National Curriculum (Key Stages 1 and 2) and religious education, particularly but not only towards the end of Key Stage 2. The notion of primary teachers' subject expertise and how it might be supported to transact the full range of curriculum requirements had to be revised. The publication of Curriculum Organisation and Classroom Practice in Primary Schools (see Chapter 13) contributed to that review. This chapter written in 1993 distin- guishes between different forms of subject expertise, and outlines different ways in which that expertise might be deployed to support and complement (not replace) the generalist role of the class teacher. It has been revised to take account of recent developments.

Currently, there are trends towards more flexible forms of staff deployment to capitalize on existing staff subject expertise, including semi-specialist and specialist teaching, and towards more developed forms of subject consultancy to support generalist class teachers. It is interesting to speculate whether this will continue with the emergence of what I have termed the ITEMS (IT, English, maths and science) curriculum which does not require the breadth of subject expertise demanded by earlier forms of the National Curriculum. Will specialist teaching, for example, wane? Will only the coordinators of ITEMS subjects have well-developed subject consul- tancy roles, along with the non-contact time and executive responsibility needed for their effective implementation?

Content

The culture of primary education continues to change. It has always been subject to change: contemporary primary schools are far removed from the newly established primary schools of the late 1940s and 1950s and they in turn were different from the elementary schools of the late nineteenth century. However, very recently the pressures for change have been forcefully articulated in the public arena and have stemmed from both professional and political sources. Such pressures have resulted particularly from the introduction of the National Curriculum with its core and other foundation subjects, from central government's determination to raise standards, from its concern to ensure 'value for money' spent on education and from its resolve to make schools more responsive to the concerns of parents and employers. The Education Acts of 1988, 1992 and 1993 have both generated, and in part reflected, these pressures. Primary schools have been, and are being, challenged to review long-held assumptions and long-practised procedures, including those related to curriculum organization, staff deployment and pedagogy.

One major theme has been to urge primary schools to make optimum use of available subject expertise through staff deployment — an issue going back at least as far as the Plowden Report of 1967. More recently, for example, early in 1992, the authors of the discussion paper, *Curriculum Organisation and Classroom Practice in Primary Schools* (Alexander et al., 1992), stressed that in the light of demands now being made on primary schools 'the problem of shortage of subject expertise is an acute one in primary education' and recommended 'the introduction of semi-specialist and specialist teaching to primary schools to strengthen the existing roles of class teacher and consultant' (p. 2). In its advice to the Secretary of State in January 1993, the National Curriculum Council argued that 'serious and urgent attention' should be given to the greater use of 'subject teachers' if the requirements of the National Curriculum were to be effectively met (p. 3). The same month, in a letter to headteachers of primary schools, the Secretary of State for Education wished schools to address the issue of the 'greater use of specialist or semi-specialist teaching' as part of his drive to raise standards. But what is meant by 'subject expertise' in the context of primary education? What is the distinction between 'specialist' and 'semi-specialist' teaching and how do these modes of staff deployment relate to subject expertise? Is there a sufficiently clear and understood common language in which to debate these issues? This paper seeks to clarify the notion of 'subject expertise' and to analyse the various ways in which that expertise is deployed in primary schools.

What Constitutes 'Subject Expertise'?

The terms 'subject expertise' and 'subject specialism' and their derivatives ('subject experts' and 'subject specialists') all appear in current discussion about staff deployment in primary schools. The two terms and their derivatives are usually used interchangeably, except by those who detect a 'secondary school' connotation to the notion of 'specialism' and who wish to avoid implying that secondary school patterns of staff deployment should be, or might be, applied in primary schools. However, to all intents and purposes the terms are synonymous.

Having expertise in a subject is relatively easy to characterize in general terms. Firstly it involves possessing knowledge and understanding of the structures, principles, processes and content of a subject, i.e. subject content knowledge. It also involves the possession of applied subject knowledge and curriculum knowledge (see Chapter 15). But how developed does that knowledge and understanding of a subject have to be to constitute 'expertise' in the context of teaching the National Curriculum to primary school pupils?

Here, a *minimum* view of what that 'expertise' consists of is stipulated and some consequences of that stipulation are explored. In the context of primary school teaching, subject content knowledge (of at least a minimum kind) involves knowledge and understanding of the structure, principles, processes and content of a subject at or beyond that embodied in an A level or its equivalent. That expertise, however, can be strongly or weakly developed.

As a general rule the extent to which subject content knowledge is strongly or weakly developed is likely to be related to the nature of the course or courses of study in that subject undertaken by an individual teacher prior to taking up a first teaching post or thereafter. Very strongly developed subject content knowledge is likely, for example, to be associated with a first degree (professionally oriented or otherwise) where the subject is the sole, or at least a prominent, component; with a higher degree focusing wholly or in part on that subject, or with an advanced diploma with a strong subject dimension. Less strongly developed subject content knowledge is likely to be associated with the study of one or two main subjects as part of two- or three-year teachers' certificate courses. Less strong still would be knowledge acquired through the study of a subject to A level and not beyond.[1] This linkage of subject content knowledge to the form of a course of study does not, of course, take into account the extent of success achieved in that course: an ordinary degree in a subject may well represent more weakly developed content knowledge than a distinction in the main subject of a teachers' certificate. It does not take into account how much time has elapsed since the knowledge was acquired; for example, knowledge in the physical sciences (and especially skills in information technology) acquired ten or so years ago may be outdated in key respects and thus less strongly developed in relation to contemporary needs than appears at first sight. Importantly, too, the linkage does not do justice to the undoubted subject content knowledge that can develop from a long-term enthusiasm pursued, for example, through extensive private reading, attendance at inservice courses and/or participation in adult education classes leading to no recognized qualification.

The knowledge and understanding of the structure, processes and content of a subject, whether strongly or weakly developed, are not directly and straightforwardly transferred from the minds of a teacher who possesses them to the minds of children who do not. The teacher needs to know *how* to apply that subject expertise to the task of teaching. Such applied subject knowledge involves, for example, knowing how to 'translate' concepts, principles and processes into terms that pupils can understand; knowing how to sequence and organize the content to be taught; knowing what to assess and how to assess it; knowing what resources are appropriate and where they can be obtained; and so on. As a general rule there is likely to be a relationship between the application dimension of subject expertise and the nature of the course or courses of study undertaken by primary teachers. Expertise with a strong application dimension is likely to be associated with a professionally oriented first degree where subject study involves a substantial component devoted to its application; with higher degrees in subject-related areas such as science or mathematical education; with advanced diplomas in subjects or aspects of subjects such as the teaching of reading; with extended inservice courses such as '20 day' designated courses for subject coordinators; and perhaps with extensive professional components related to main subjects in teachers' certificate courses. A weaker application dimension to subject expertise is likely to result from most, if not all, generalist primary PGCE courses. Study of a subject to A level has no built-in subject application knowledge. As before, this linkage does not do justice to the strongly applied subject knowledge that can accrue from attendance at a host of short inservice courses over a professional career, active membership of a subject association, extensive private reading and the sheer experience of teaching a subject, and reflecting on that teaching, over a number of years.

The Deployment of Subject Expertise

Subject expertise, however strongly or weakly developed, is deployed in primary schools in two ways. First, it is put to use through the teaching of a class of children or a number of classes,[2] i.e. *subject-specialist teaching*. Second, subject specialism may be put to use in helping other teachers teach a subject more effectively, i.e. *subject specialist consultancy*. Though not always realized in practice, such consultancy is now a common expectation in the vast majority of primary schools. Subject specialist teaching and consultancy are often linked but are not necessarily so.

Subject Specialist Teaching

In an attempt to bring greater clarity to the notion of 'subject specialist teaching', four modes are distinguished here, each based on existing practice in primary schools. Paradoxically the first mode is the most common, yet the most unacknowledged; and the last is the least common yet the one which raises most concerns amongst those committed to generalist class teaching in primary education.

1. *Class subject-specialist teaching*: subject expertise can be deployed by a class teacher in teaching that subject or those subjects to the children in their own class. In these terms, all primary pupils receive subject specialist teaching for some parts of the curriculum from their class teachers. In one or two subjects that teaching is likely to be informed by strongly developed subject expertise (varying in the strength of its application dimension) and deriving in particular from the course or courses of study undertaken previously by the class teacher. There will, however, be some subjects or aspects of the curriculum where the teacher cannot draw on subject expertise (even at its minimum) but these may be rather fewer in number than commonly acknowledged in discussions about 'the lack of subject expertise'. There is no necessary dichotomy between subject

specialist teaching and generalist class teaching. Primary teachers can, and do, both to varying degrees! A key issue for school management is not whether this form of specialist teaching should take place — it inevitably will — but how far it should be capitalized upon and made an explicit feature of school policy. For example, how far should individual class teachers be encouraged (or even required) to delve more deeply or widely in those subjects in which they have considerable expertise? If this happens, should headteachers take steps to ensure that as far as possible over their school career children receive a variety of subject specialisms from their classteachers?

2. *Exchange subject specialist teaching*: subject expertise can be deployed by a class teacher to teach that subject or those subjects to the class of a colleague on an exchange basis. Where both teachers deploy their subject specialism to the other's class, both classes receive subject specialist teaching. However, it is important to distinguish 'full-blown' exchange subject specialist teaching from a partial version where a teacher takes another's class not in order to deploy their own subject expertise but simply to release that teacher to deploy theirs. Particularly since the introduction of the National Curriculum, exchange subject specialist teaching has become more common, as has its partial version. It is certainly administratively convenient and requires no extra staffing costs. A key issue for headteachers is how far the exchange provides subject specialist teaching for *both* of the classes involved or whether only one class receives the benefit.

3. *Semi-specialist subject teaching*: an individual teacher's subject expertise can be deployed not only for their own class or a colleague's class on an exchange basis but also for two or more classes other than their own. Such a teacher is a semi-specialist provided that he or she does not teach that subject or those subjects exclusively. It is this form of staff deployment that primary schools have been urged to consider introducing, especially at Key Stage 2, as they seek to meet the requirements of the National Curriculum. Some are responding positively as indicated by an OFSTED report published early in 1993: 'The small but significant number of primary schools engaged in a measure of semi-specialist teaching constitutes a significant bridge-head and one that is likely to grow, albeit slowly within current staffing constraints' (OFSTED, 1993, pp. 18–19). A key management issue for headteachers is the effects of the semi-specialist's deployment on the work of her own class. It is important that the class's programme of work is managed by one person to provide an appropriate degree of challenge across the curriculum and to avoid undue fragmentation as other teachers 'fill in' for the semi-specialist.

4. *Fully specialist subject teaching*: an individual teacher's subject expertise can be deployed to teach that subject or those subjects exclusively to a considerable number of classes, though not necessarily all, in a primary school. In reality, partly because of logistical difficulties associated with the size of primary schools and partly because of ideological objections to

'secondary style' patterns of staff deployment, very few primary schools in the maintained sector can, or do, employ full-time staff in specialist teaching, though part-time teachers are sometimes used in this way for aspects such as music or special needs.

The main criterion which needs to be used in judging whether or not to employ some or all of these modes of subject specialist teaching is how far that deployment provides the challenging teaching required to give pupils full access to the range of curriculum requirements appropriate to their developing abilities. Headteachers need to consider what mode or modes best promote higher quality and standards in their own contexts. They also need to monitor, evaluate and modify the results of their decisions as circumstances change — and inevitably they will.

Subject Specialist Consultancy

As with subject expertise itself, subject specialist consultancy can be strongly or weakly developed — depending on factors such as the management structure of the school; the school's policy for staff deployment and staff development; and the individual interests, expertise and influence of subject consultants (or coordinators). Depending on the strength of its development, consultancy involves individuals drawing on their subject expertise to work at all or some of the following activities:

- preparing policies and complementary schemes of work for the school in consultation with the rest of the staff;
- providing guidance and support to other members of staff in planning, implementing and evaluating the scheme of work, based on informed consultation, meetings and working alongside individual teachers;
- obtaining and organizing teaching resources;
- monitoring and evaluating work and policy implementation in the subject through the school;
- overseeing the assessment and recording of pupils' progress;
- helping colleagues to diagnose and remediate children's learning difficulties;
- attending relevant INSET and arranging INSET (school-based or otherwise) for members of staff;
- liaison with schools from which children come and to which they go, and also with LEA personnel.

It is important to recognize that subject specialist consultancy is not necessarily associated with subject specialist teaching; the two are conceptually and practically distinct. It is possible, for example, for subject consultancy to be well developed without the individual participating in any of the modes of specialist teaching identified above: heads who act as coordinators for a subject but do not actually teach that subject illustrate this. Similarly, it is possible for a subject consultant to be effective even though they teach only their own class through a combination of subject specialist class teaching and generalist class teaching. From recent inspection evidence (OFSTED, 1997), it seems likely that the impact of subject specialist consultancy is enhanced by an association with subject specialist teaching (in modes 2–4).

A Common Language

Current discussion about curriculum organization, staff deployment and pedagogy instigated by *Curriculum Organisation and Classroom Practice in Primary Schools*, is important to the ongoing development of primary education in England. However, for that discussion to be productive nationally, it needs to be conducted in a common language which embodies clear distinctions reflecting the realities of primary schools. This paper attempts to make such distinctions and provides appropriate terminology which could be used to inform discussion of staff deployment in primary schools and, in particular, to explore issues such as the extent to which there *is* a shortage of subject expertise, how that expertise might be recognized, how teachers might be encouraged to acknowledge and exploit it, and how it might be deployed to teach a reconstituted primary curriculum for the benefit of the children themselves.

Notes

1 It is important to acknowledge that however strongly or weakly developed, subject expertise will vary in terms of its direct relevance to teaching primary-aged children. To take two extreme examples, a first degree involving extensive study of medieval English is likely to be far less relevant to primary teaching than the A level study of geography or history.
2 It can also be deployed to teach smaller groups of pupils.

References

ALEXANDER, R. et al. (1992) *Curriculum Organisation and Classroom Practice in Primary Schools*, London: DFE.
NATIONAL CURRICULUM COUNCIL (1993) *The National Curriculum at Key Stages 1 and 2*, London: NCC.
OFSTED (1993) *Curriculum Organisation and Classroom Practice in Primary Schools: A Follow-up Report*, London: OFSTED.
OFSTED (1997) *Using Subject Specialists to Promote High Standards at Key Stage 2: An Illustrative Survey*, London: OFSTED.

Part 4

Primary Teacher Education

17   The National Curriculum for Primary ITT: A Key Stage 6 Core Curriculum?

Looking back it was inevitable that sooner or later a national curriculum for initial teacher training *(note the term) would follow the introduction of the National Curriculum for schools. As this chapter, written in 1997, indicates, there are some similarities between the two curricula: the development of both by quangos; the same emphasis on the core subjects; the vain attempt to pin down curricular requirements in unambiguous language; the emphasis on content; the lack of any rationale; the use of working parties working in isolation from one another to draw up proposals; the lack of consultation with those in the sector; and the impossibly tight timescale for meaningful implementation. There was the same political 'spin' surrounding their introduction: not Kenneth Baker seeking an Education Reform Act to drastically raise standards and enhance his personal reputation but Gillian Shepherd seeking to be tough on teacher trainers (whilst softening her attitude to teachers) and being 'bounced' into action through the agency of a chief inspector making much of OFSTED's report into the teaching of reading in three inner London LEAs. There were also some differences: the equivalent of an ITEMS-based curriculum for initial teacher training, no assessment arrangements (as least as yet) but rigid reinforcement through a very problematic OFSTED inspection regime.*

Introduction

Sixteen years ago there was no National Curriculum. Within the constraints of professional and public opinion, primary schools were free to determine their own curricula except for the legal requirement to teach 'religious instruction' (widely disregarded in practice). There was no national system for the assessment of pupils and no pressure from the centre to adopt particular teaching methods, ways of grouping or modes of curriculum organization.

Sixteen years ago higher education institutions and departments concerned with initial teacher education (ITE) were free to determine the content and methodology of their courses provided they met the requirements of the universities or the Council for National Academic Awards who validated their courses and qualifications and who held academic freedom as sacrosanct.

Sixteen years ago central government had no means of influencing curricular provision in ITE except indirectly through the professional advice offered by Her Majesty's Inspectors, themselves free from the necessity to adhere to any particular policy. At that time, partly as a result of reports from HMI, central government was increasingly conscious and concerned at the diversity of provision within both school education and ITE, the relevance of that provision to what it deemed 'the world of work' and the wide differences in the quality of education provided in different schools and institutions. In what in retrospect seems an unduly timorous way central government was stirring itself to intervene decisively into what was seen as two 'secret gardens' one tended by primary school 'gardeners' and the other by higher education 'horticulturists'.

Sixteen years on, English primary schools are required to follow a National Curriculum of ten subjects plus locally determined religious education. This curriculum, especially in the 'core' subjects of mathematics and English and the rather lesser 'core' subjects of science and information technology, is more closely prescribed than similar curricula in many other countries. National systems of pupil assessment and school inspection have been instituted, in part, to provide central government with data on standards of attainment and quality of provision. There is powerful pressure (as yet just short of legislation) from the centre to adopt particular (politically correct?) forms of curriculum organization, grouping and teaching methods. The curricular (and less the pedagogic) world of primary schools has changed dramatically.

Sixteen years on, higher education institutions and departments concerned with initial teacher training (ITT) have to provide courses which meet not only the requirements of validating universities but also multiple, ever-more tightly prescribed criteria laid down by central government. They are subject to almost continuous inspection by HMI working under the auspices of a non-ministerial government department, the Office for Standards in Education (OFSTED). Their reports are made available to a governmental agency, the Teacher Training Agency (TTA) which, amongst other matters, has the responsibility 'to secure a diversity of high quality and cost-effective initial teacher training which ensures that new teachers have the knowledge, understanding and skills to teach pupils effectively' (TTA Corporate Plan, 1996, p. 12). It was the TTA who, nine years after the establishment of the National Curriculum for schools, proposed the introduction of the Initial Teacher Training National Curriculum for primary English and for primary mathematics from September 1997 and for primary science and IT from a later date — a kind of 'Key Stage 6 core curriculum' for intending primary school teachers. That curriculum was incorporated into Circulars 10/97 and 4/98 setting out 'a full and detailed codification of requirements for new teachers'.

The National Curriculum for Primary Initial Teacher Training: An Overview

In introducing the National Curriculum for Primary Initial Teacher Training and other standards for the award of qualified teacher status, Anthea Millett, the chief executive of the TTA, pointed out that 'It is the first time ever that we in education have set down clearly and explicitly what we expect of our new teachers, in terms of what they must know, understand and be able to do' (1997, p. 12). Never before has central government described in such detailed 'black and white' the knowledge and understanding *trainees* (note the term) need in order to develop pupils' competence in English, mathematics, science and IT; the teaching and assessment methods they are to use; and the knowledge and understanding of the subject matter they need to underpin their teaching. The proposals herald a sea-change in teacher education/training similar to that experienced in schools with the implementation of the National Curriculum after the Education Reform Act of 1988.

Whatever the merits of the National Curriculum for Initial Teacher Training (and it does have merits), there are a number of general points which raise important issues for both teacher education and the teaching profession in general. Much *could* be made of the way in which the proposals were produced, such as anonymous working groups operating to an impossibly tight timescale and in consequence not involving adequate consultation during the drafting process. However, here more substantive issues of curriculum design and structure are raised.

Most fundamentally, the TTA has not provided any rationale for the curriculum. No statement of purposes has been provided; no reasons have been offered for the content prescribed; no attempt has been made to discuss the nature and purpose of the English, mathematics, science or ICT that intending primary teachers are to teach. There has been no attempt to 'locate' the proposed training curricula in relation to either the curriculum followed by students in school prior to their training or to the process of induction or continuing professional development following it. The proposals are presented as straightforward educational 'common sense' in no need of justification and self-evidently 'right' for the next generation of primary teachers. Neither providers nor trainees are expected, let alone encouraged, to question their basis. Perhaps the proposals are 'right' but not entirely so? There is a direct parallel with the National Curriculum for schools; it too has been provided with no detailed rationale apart from the highly general, vague clauses of Section 1 of the Education Reform Act. The key questions remain: Why this particular set of detailed proposals? What are they designed to do? Are they appropriate as parts of higher education courses where, presumably, students are to be encouraged to question and challenge rather than meekly accept educational 'common sense'?

The design of the proposed National Curricula is instructive. There is only one element: a detailed specification of the content to be taught which is provided in a valuably detailed and direct form. Apart from the inevitable ambiguities inherent in the English language and the scope for a degree of diverse interpretation they provide, the proposals set out a reasonably clear and useful programme of work. Interestingly, the structure and terminology of the school National Curriculum are avoided: there are no attainment targets, no reference to programmes of study, and no assessment arrangements and 'levels'. The absence of assessment requirements is particularly noteworthy. There are formidable problems related to the valid, reliable assessment of teaching competences or standards, but as Richard Daughtery (1997) points out 'The National Curriculum for ITT neatly side-steps such problems by not having an assessment model at all'. Why is the proposed structure of the ITT curriculum so different from that of the school curriculum? Is the government or, at the very least, the TTA unhappy with the latter? Does this presage a change following the curriculum review currently being conducted by the Qualifications and Curriculum Authority? Are the proposed curricula for teacher training 'throw-backs' or 'throw-forwards'?

The curricula are intended to cover only the 'core' subjects of English, mathematics, science and ICT, though other parts of Circulars 10/97 and 4/98, concerned with the standards required for qualified teacher status, have many implications for other aspects of training courses. Anthea Millett argues: 'We have set out the priorities, the core elements of what we believe initial teacher training should cover . . . There is still plenty of scope for flexibility, variation and innovation.' No-one would deny the importance of the core subjects but why is there no intention to spell out the training requirements of the remaining subjects of the school National Curriculum and of religious education? Are there no essential elements in these subjects which all teacher-trainees ought to be taught? Is this yet another manifestation of the current political obsession with so-called 'basics' and the education system's supposed neglect of these?

By concentrating only on the 'core', by specifying this in detail and by not prescribing the length of such courses in those subjects, the TTA has left providers of initial teacher training with extremely difficult, perhaps intractable, problems of fitting curricular quarts into narrow-necked, regularly inspected pint bottles. Nor do the proposals take due account of the very different contexts (especially constraints) of one-year postgraduate courses (involving a maximum of 20 weeks tuition) and three- or four-year initial degree courses. Especially in relation to the very short PGCE courses, are there the necessary 'degrees of freedom' to promote the innovation and flexibility trumpeted in the TTA's rhetoric? The very detail of the proposals — one of their strengths — serves to exacerbate design problems. The difficulties schools faced when attempting to manage the over-prescriptive, unmanageable pre-Dearing National Curriculum are in danger of being paralleled in the initial training sector.

A Necessary Ongoing Debate

Whatever the merits or de-merits of the current National Curriculum for ITT, the debate of which it is a part will continue — not just the officially sponsored debate about the content of initial training courses and the roles, responsibilities and accountabilities of the various providers and agencies, but also the more fundamental debate about the purpose and nature of teacher *education* or *training* with its focus on the kinds of teachers needed to educate future generations. Does Britain need an army of *basic instructors* to staff its primary schools and inculcate pupils with necessary skills and knowledge? If so, the current National Curriculum for primary ITT could, pared down, provide the instruction needed for the instructors. Does Britain need a cadre of *skilled technicians* able to deliver the school National Curriculum programmes of study to pupils in an efficient and effective way? If so, the current training curriculum has the makings of a very useful and detailed training manual for would-be technicians. Or does Britain need a profession of imaginative, creative teachers whose informed professional judgment leads to intelligent action? If so, the proposed training curriculum will *not* suffice as it stands. It lacks imagination and vision. It embodies, rather than opens up to scrutiny, a straight forward, value-free common-sense view of education, teaching, English, mathematics, science and ICT. Its simplistic approach belies the complexity of the educational enterprise whether in school or college. It will certainly provide would-be teachers with important knowledge and skills but it will fail to provide them with the understanding, or to develop *with* them the necessary attitudes and values, which they need to make *educational* judgments and undertake intelligent action to foster their children's learning. It *will* provide a Key Stage 6 curriculum but not one which, to quote Section 1 of the ERA, 'promotes the spiritual, moral, cultural, mental and physical development' of future teachers.

References

DAUGHERTY, R. (1997) 'Bright ideas that will lead to a primary shortage', *The Times Educational Supplement*, 11 April.
MILLETT, A. (1997) 'Bringing a new professionalism into teaching', *Education Journal*, March.

18   Primary Teacher Education: High Status? High Standards? — A Personal Response to Recent Initiatives

This chapter, written in 1997, demonstrates that primary teacher education has been, and still is, the subject of considerable criticism in official quarters. Despite the very largely positive picture painted of the sector in OFSTED inspection reports in survey after survey, the criticism remains. Teacher education is seen to be implicated in the general underperformance of the primary sector, despite no convincing evidence from OFSTED, international studies or English research agencies to support that view of underperformance. So much of the discussion about both primary education and primary teacher education is underpinned by utilitarian overtones, more redolent of the values of the nineteenth than of the twenty-first century and needing critical examination. There is also being propagated a strong belief in a consensual view of 'good' or 'best' practice, presumably as defined by the official bodies themselves, rather than by the teaching force in schools or in higher education. There is also a strong, uncritical reliance on the findings of school effectiveness research — a newly established 'tradition' which I believe has yet to produce findings which rise much above the commonplace. Throughout current discussion in official quarters there is an unwillingness to confront the complex, uncertain, value-laden, interpersonal nature of teaching. Despite views to the contrary, teaching is not, and cannot be, a form of applied pedagogic mechanics.

Wonderland?

'When we were little,' the Mock Turtle went on at last, more calmly, though sobbing a little now and then, 'we went to school in the sea' . . .
'I only took the regular course.'
'What was that?' inquired Alice.
'Reeling and Writhing, of course, to begin with,' the Mock Turtle replied, 'and then the different branches of Arithmetic — Ambition, Distraction, Uglification and Derision.' (Carroll, 1995, pp. 93–4)

These have been, and remain, major components of the core curriculum for initial teacher education (ITE) and for primary education for some years before, and now after, the publication of the 1997 White Paper, *Excellence in Schools*, and of Circulars 10/97 and 4/98, *Teaching: High Status, High Standards*. Uglification and derision have characterized public pronouncements of both sectors, particularly before and, to some extent after, the 1997 General Election. Though not based on even reasonably conclusive evidence, criticisms of English primary schools for failing to teach 'basic skills' effectively have also been used to castigate training institutions. Tellingly, the TTA's announcement in 1996 of its determination to move towards a National Curriculum for Initial Teacher Training took place in the context of a critical (and later much criticized) OFSTED inspection report on the teaching of reading in three inner-London LEAs (1996) (Mortimore and Goldstein, 1996; Richards, 1997). Practice in primary ITE is not, of course, without its shortcomings but standards have been found to be mostly sound or good in inspections — an overall judgment that could be made of primary education more generally.

Why then a process of uglification? Almost certainly, part of the answer lies in ambition on the part of individuals or institutions to ensure that they or their organizations are positioned to play robust parts in the 'driving up' of standards both in schools and in ITE. The result is 'reeling and writhing' on a massive scale both in schools and higher education institutions. In the latter, staff are reeling with having to meet the insatiable appetite for data from a TTA bureaucracy trying desperately to understand and to regulate the teacher education sector. Even more than their colleagues in school, they are reeling with the pressures of almost continuous inspection — a massive distraction, for the most part, from their commitment to improving the quality of initial teacher preparation. Preparation for inspection, the long drawn-out inspection process itself, and coping with the aftermath are all taking tolls — on staff morale, on preparation time for teaching (whatever happened to research?) and on links with schools and mentors, as well as on rainforests, printers and printing ink. The 'high status' nature of inspections with personal and institutional futures at stake results in acute mental discomfort (one definition of 'writhing'); a resignation to play the game by OFSTED's rules (while often being uncertain about their changing nature); an unwillingness to express public dissent from a deeply flawed and unfair inspection regime; and a determination to hide from inspectors, both HMI and attached inspectors, problems and difficulties which a more sensitive, less punitive, inspection and advisory system might help resolve. Similar issues arise in relation to school inspections.

Rhetoric

The picture painted above draws parallels between the current predicament of primary ITE and of primary education itself. This paper attempts to draw further parallels — occasioned by the publication of the Education White Paper, *Excellence in Schools* (DFEE, 1997a), and *Circulars 10/97* and *4/98, Teaching: High Status, High Standards* (DFEE, 1997b, 1998). These documents are intended to improve quality of education and to raise both standards and the status of teachers but both need to have their assumptions analysed, their language contested and their proposals critiqued.

At one level those involved in initial teacher preparation are not in dispute with the Government, the DFEE or the TTA. There is virtually universal support for the Government's 'determination to raise standards across the education system and to ensure that all pupils have access to the high quality teaching they deserve' (DFEE, 1997b, p. 3). There is widespread support, too, for the need to give priority to primary education and to raising standards of literacy and numeracy. Similarly, those involved in initial teacher preparation would agree that 'to raise the standards we expect of schools and teachers, we must raise the standards we expect of new teachers' (*ibid*). But such statements are rhetorical and such support is rhetorical. Such propositions are the educational equivalent of virtue, motherhood and apple pie. Would anyone seriously advocate their opposites? Policy for both primary and teacher education needs to be built on a firmer foundation than rhetoric; this chapter contends that there are fundamental problems with some of the assumptions on which policy is being based.

Assumptions

Unsatisfactory Standards

The first major assumption is that 'standards' in both primary and teacher education are unsatisfactory in a very significant proportion of institutions. In relation to primary schools that assumption was made explicit some years ago in HMCI's Annual Report for 1994–95 where it was controversially stated that 'it is evident that overall standards of pupil achievement need to be raised in about half of primary schools' (OFSTED, 1996, p. 8). The criticism, though more muted, continued in the next Annual Report: 'About two-fifths of the schools have some strengths but they also have weaknesses that hamper the achievement of higher standards . . . Overall standards are judged to be poor in about one in 12 schools in Key Stage 1 and one in six in Key Stage 2. Standards in these schools need to be substantially improved' (OFSTED, 1997, p. 11). This down-beat assessment of primary standards is the implicit backcloth for the 1997 White Paper's assertion that 'Excellence at the top is not matched by high standards for the majority of children' who are judged to be 'not achieving their potential' (p. 10). The assumption is one of considerable underperformance by schools.

In relation to teacher education, OFSTED's overall assessments have been rather more positive, though still guarded, as claimed in the 1994–95 Annual Report: 'Early indications are that the training of students to teach mathematics and English and to conduct assessment and recording in primary schools is sound in the majority of HEIs and that it is often good. In a significant minority of cases, however, there are shortcomings related to students' competences in school' (OFSTED, 1996, p. 62). In the report no indication is given as to what 'the majority' means (51 per cent, 99 per cent?) or how large the 'significant minority' might be (5 per cent, 49 per cent?). The following year's Annual Report implicates teacher education in the moral panic over standards in numeracy and literacy: 'serious concerns continue to be expressed about standards of numeracy and literacy, and, indeed, about how well students are trained' (OFSTED, 1997, p. 7). This criticism becomes more muted in the 1997 White Paper but is presupposed by the claims that 'we must raise the standards we expect of new teachers' and that 'Improving the skills of our new teachers in these areas is critical to achieving our numeracy and literacy targets' (DFEE, 1997, p. 47).

In relation to primary schools how can such a negative picture be reconciled with other evidence that in 1995–96:

- standards of achievement were judged satisfactory or better in 95% of sessions in nursery schools and classes and in 93% of reception classes;
- in Key Stage 1 standards were satisfactory or better in 87% of lessons;
- in Key Stage 2 standards were satisfactory in 83% of lessons;
- the quality of teaching was good or very good in 41% of lessons and satisfactory or better in 83%?

Such figures give no cause for complacency but nor do they suggest that standards in 'a significant minority' of primary schools give serious cause for concern.

OFSTED has not published or made available any comparable data on standards or the quality of teaching in teacher education despite its extensive database. It is crucially important for the future of the teacher education community that it persuades the government in its 'new spirit of openness' to pressurize OFSTED into releasing the aggregate data from the Primary Follow Up Survey so that the data can be debated and its significance assessed rather than the sector having only to rely on, and react to, OFSTED's or the TTA's, summary interpretation of what the data reveal.

Unfavourable International Comparisons

A second assumption is that standards of attainment in English primary schools compare unfavourably with those in our 'competitor' countries and that inevitably initial teacher education is implicated in that relative failure. This general overall assumption is made explicit in relation to numeracy and literacy in the White Paper:

- too many children have poor literacy and numeracy skills;
- we have fallen behind many other developed countries in numeracy;
- our performance in literacy is behind a number of comparable English-speaking countries. (DFEE, 1997a, p. 19)

Putting aside the enormous methodological problems surrounding comparative studies of educational achievement, well summarized by Reynolds and Farrell (1996), it needs to be stressed that there have been no such studies conducted for most areas of the primary curriculum — history, geography, design technology, information technology, art, music, physical education or religious education. For English there has been only one study involving English primary-aged pupils — in written composition conducted in 1984–85 — but subject to severe methodological problems. Over the last quarter of a century no international surveys of reading attainment at primary level involving English pupils have been undertaken. It is impossible to see how research findings can possibly support at primary level the claim in the third point above.

Two studies conducted in the 1990s into children's achievement in mathematics have received considerable attention in the media, have underpinned the criticisms in the White Paper, and have contributed, more indirectly, to the decision to introduce the National Curriculum for Primary Initial Teacher Training. Both Foxman (1992) and Keys (1997) focus on the performance of 9-year-olds (note *only* that age group) and both reveal overall lower than average performance compared with most other Western European countries as well as states such as Taiwan and Korea. However, as Keys (1997) points out, this lower than average performance characterized some areas of mathematics such as number operations but not others: '9-year-olds in England, together with those in Australia and Hong Kong, came "top" in geometry and . . . scored above the international mean score on data representation and analysis' (p. 20). Interestingly, other comparative data published in 1997 showed English 13-year-old pupils scoring well above average in the application of number to everyday problems. English pupils may be less proficient at number operations than their counterparts in many countries but they appear to be far better at applying their knowledge in real-life contexts. Are these findings sufficient to fuel the moral panic behind the proposed numeracy strategy and the detailed requirements of the NC for Primary ITT?

Such reservations are given extra force by the results of two similar surveys (Foxman, 1992) and (Keys, 1997) also carried out in the 1990s into 9-year-olds' performance in science which showed well above average results despite the tests focusing on scientific knowledge and understanding rather than scientific investigation, a major component of the English primary science curriculum. Why then the necessity for a very detailed prescriptive NC for ITT in primary science? Shouldn't initial teacher education be implicated in the success, rather than in the failure, of primary science? Or is the assumption of the comparative failure of English primary and teacher education too deeply embedded in the collective psychology of the DFEE, OFSTED and the TTA?

Unexamined Language

The language of the White Paper, of Circulars 10/97 and 4/98 and of the TTA is instructive in uncovering further assumptions about the purpose of primary (and thus teacher) education and about the nature of teaching.

In relation to what it calls 'the foundations of learning' the White Paper is clear and unequivocal:

> Investment in learning in the 21st century, is the equivalent of investment in the machinery and technical innovation that was essential to the first great industrial

revolution. Then it was physical capital; now it is human capital. We need to build up the store of knowledge and keep abreast of rapid technological development if we are to prepare the future generation. Our children are our future as a civilised society and a prosperous nation. If they are to have an education that matches the best in the world, we must start now to lay the foundations, by getting integrated early years education and childcare, and primary education, right.

Note the language of economics: of 'investment', 'technical innovation', 'capital', 'store of knowledge', 'technological development', 'prosperous nation'. Why these particular guiding metaphors? Why the emphasis on an economic rather than a personal or cultural calculus? The importance of primary education to the economy is at best indirect and partial (despite supposed evidence from competitor countries) so why emphasize the economic dimension at the expense of others? The assumptions behind the use of such language need debating by the education community, though such issues form no part of the TTA's training curriculum and are unlikely to be debated by students preparing to be teachers.

Indeed the TTA shares a similar language and similar assumptions, drawn in particular from 'the science of machinery' which is put to work for economic ends. Note the technical/mechanical nature of the language used by the TTA's Chief Executive, tellingly taken from an article entitled 'Bringing a new professionalism (sic) into teaching':

> We cannot *unlock* teachers' potential if we do not *equip* them, as part of their initial *training*, with the *toolbox* of *skills* they need to be *effective*. At the moment there is a danger that some new teachers may never even find out what *tools* are supposed to be in the *toolbox*, let alone acquire the skills to use them effectively. (Millett, 1997, p. 12, my italics)

Do the ideas of primary education as primarily economic investment and initial teacher preparation as essentially skilling-up technicians or mechanics do justice to the nature of both primary and teacher education as many practitioners conceive them? Is teaching *simply* (sic) a straightforward if complicated technical activity concerned with delivering a pre-planned curriculum with clearly defined, agreed targets rather than with the making of complex, contestable judgments and undertaking intelligent action in the complex ecology of classroom and school to foster that most intangible of outcomes — children's learning? Are there ethical, interpersonal, intellectual and cultural dimensions untouched by the use of 'economic' language? Shouldn't these dimensions also feature in any defensible NC for primary ITT?

Best Practice?

Another instructive aspect of the 1997 White Paper (DFEE, 1997a) is its frequent reference to 'good' or 'best' practice. Ironically the phrase has been resurrected by central Government and its agencies at the very time when its long-standing use in primary education has been successfully (and justifiably) challenged. In relation to teaching methods, the White Paper intones:

> We must make sure that all teachers understand the *best* methods of teaching and know how to use them. (p. 9)

> All primary teachers need to know how to teach reading in line with *proven best* practice. (p. 19)

In terms of the curriculum:

> A good education . . . offers opportunities to gain insight into the *best* that has been thought and said and done.

In terms of partnerships:

> We shall seek to strengthen existing partnerships between schools and higher education to ensure that teacher training is firmly rooted in the *best* classroom practice. (p. 47, my italics)

And so on.

But 'best' for what? 'Best' or 'good' in respect of which set of values? 'Best' in terms of what conception of education? What is 'best' or 'good' involves value judgments, not factual generalizations, it cannot simply be asserted as self-evident without justification. The use of 'best' or 'good' practice in the White Paper implies a straightforward, value-free view of education, presumably based on the 'common-sense' view of the Government and its agencies.

Proven Research?

Unlike its predecessor which placed almost no reliance on educational research, the new government seems far too wedded to its supposed benefits. The honeymoon with school improvement and school effectiveness research may not last long but at present at least the DfEE, the Standards and Effectiveness Unit and, to a lesser extent, the TTA seem to assume that the keys to educational improvement are value-free (see previous section), clear and 'proven' through research. Notions such as 'proven best practice' are used to make claims which many educational researchers would disavow. There is no hint in the official literature that research findings are at best suggestive; are never definitive; and are valuable, not as blue-prints to effective practice, but as sources of useful insights and possible lines of enquiry or practice to pursue. The notion of research or inspection providing clear 'proven' answers ties in with a technicist approach to teaching — research as a kind of applied pedagogic mechanics establishing 'what works' and what does not.

Hard Times?

This chapter has attempted a critique of some of the assumptions underlying, recent official pronouncements about primary education and teacher education. Though in Circulars 10/97 and 4/98 the notion of 'competence' (with its utilitarian, down-beat overtones) has been replaced by that of 'standard' (with its qualitative, up-beat overtones) the notion of teaching as a value-free if complicated technical activity remains the dominant assumption. With its embodiment in the standards required for qualified teacher status it represents not the re-professionalization, but the *de*-professionalization, of teaching. Official views are informed by a Victorian model of training concerned with 'turning out' technicians rather than embryonic professionals.

This chapter began with a quotation from a Victorian classic, *Alice in Wonderland*. It ends in *Hard Times* with Dickens' description of the *training*, received by Mr Choakcumchild, close in terms and, amazingly close in terms of some of its English content, to that expected of current 'trainees':

> He and some 140 other school masters had been turned out at the same time, in the same factory, like so many pianoforte legs. He had been put through an immense variety of paces and had answered volumes of head-breaking questions. Orthography, etymology, syntax and prosody, biography, astronomy, geography and general cosmology, the sciences of compound proportion, algebra, land-surveying and levelling, vocal music, and drawing from models were all at the ends of his ten chilled fingers. He had worked his stony way into Her Majesty's most Honourable Privy Council's Schedule B, and had taken the bloom off the higher branches of mathematics and physical science, French, German, Latin and Greek. He knew all about the Water Sheds of all the world (whatever they are) and all the histories of all the peoples, and all the names of all the rivers and mountains, and the productions, manners and customs of all the countries, and all their boundaries and bearings on the two-and-thirty points of the compass.

Very tellingly, (prescient of the current obsession with 'subject knowledge' perhaps) he concludes:

> If he had only learnt a little less, how infinitely better he might have taught much more. (Dickens, 1994, p. 7)

References

CARROLL, L. (1995) *The Penguin Selected Works of Lewis Carroll*, London: Claremont Books.

DEPARTMENT FOR EDUCATION AND EMPLOYMENT (DFEE) (1997a) *Excellence in Schools*, London, Her Majesty's Stationery Office.

DEPARTMENT FOR EDUCATION AND EMPLOYMENT (DFEE) (1997b) *Requirements for Courses of Initial Teacher Training*, Circular 10/97, London: DfEE.

DEPARTMENT FOR EDUCATION AND EMPLOYMENT (DfEE) *Teaching: High Status, High Standards*, Circular 4/98, London: DfEE.

DICKENS, C. (1994) *Hard Times*, Harmondsworth: Penguin Books.

FOXMAN, D. (1992) *Learning Mathematics and Science (The Second International Assessment of Educational Progress in England)*, National Foundation for Educational Research.

KEYS, W. (1997) 'Behind the headlines: What do the results of TIMMS really tell us?' *Education Journal*, September.

MILLETT, A. (1997) 'Bringing a new professionalism into teaching', *Education Journal*, March.

MORTIMORE, P. and GOLDSTEIN, H. (1996) *The Teaching of Reading in 45 Inner London Primary Schools: A Critical Examination of OFSTED Research*, London: University of London Institute of Education.

OFSTED (1996) *The Annual Report of Her Majesty's Chief Inspector of Schools: Standards and Quality in Education 1994/95*, London: HMSO.

OFSTED (1997) *The Annual Report of Her Majesty's Chief Inspector of Schools: Standards and Quality 1995/96*, London: HMSO.

REYNOLDS, D. and FARRELL, S. (1996) *Worlds Apart? A Review of International Surveys of Educational Achievement Involving England*, London: HMSO.

RICHARDS, C. (1997) *Primary Education, Standards and OFSTED: Towards a More Authentic Conversation*, Occasional Paper, Centre for Research into Elementary and Primary Education, University of Warwick.

Part 5

End-piece

19   The 'Professionalization' of Primary Teaching Under New Labour

Currently (1999) I feel uncertain and uneasy about New Labour's policies towards primary education, but it is difficult to pinpoint exactly why. The government has placed education as one of its highest priorities — that's fine. It is devoting a large amount of 'new' extra money to the education service — that's long overdue. It is recognizing the vital importance of the early years and of primary education in a way that previous governments over the past quarter of a century have signally failed to do — that's excellent. It is promoting higher standards in literacy and numeracy — that's appropriate since standards can always be, and should be, higher in these core areas of primary education. It is promoting literacy, numeracy and information and communications technology through well-funded national strategies — that's sensible. It is attempting to overcome social exclusion — that's essential, though the claims and demands made on schools' contribution to this are likely to prove far-fetched.

Then why am I uncertain and uneasy? Part of the explanation, I think, lies in the assumptions, never fully articulated, which underlie the government's attitude to primary education. Basically the 1997 White Paper, Excellence in Schools, and government initiatives following it are based on two linked assumptions. First, the education system, especially primary education, has failed to provide an acceptable standard of education, especially in the 'basics' of literacy and numeracy and therefore requires 'special measures'. Second, teachers, especially primary teachers, have held up the necessary process of improvement and provide the resistance against which, in the government's very telling rhetoric, standards have to be 'driven up'.

These assumptions need examination and debate with the primary teaching profession. They are based on an uncritical acceptance of the results of national and international testing; they appear to run counter to the detailed evidence collected school by school by OFSTED inspectors. The government and its advisers appear to have no serious doubts as to the reliability, validity and utility of national tests and as to their representativeness of all that is important in the core subjects of English, mathematics and science. They appear to have no doubts as to the validity, reliability, utility and generalizability of comparative studies of educational achievement despite the enormous methodological problems and controversies surrounding them and the absence of data at primary level of achievement in all subjects except mathematics and science. However, both the teaching profession and the academic community do have doubts and these doubts need debating before policy changes are made. It may be that the government's assumptions are justified, at least to some degree, but equally they may not be. Policy on the basis of unexamined assumption does a great disservice to the teaching profession, which the government and its agencies claim to respect and to want to enhance.

Part of my uncertainty and unease arises from the way the government is approaching its reforms. In its haste it seems to be riding roughshod over the teaching profession through a kind of 'democratic totalitarianism'. It is not consulting over the substance of its policies but only over the minutiae of their implementation. We are witnessing government of education by coercion and assertion, not by reasoned argument or by consent won through adequate consultation and through listening to what teachers have to say. To repeat an earlier point, this is not to say that its assumptions are necessarily mistaken or its policies necessarily misguided; only, that some may be, in whole or in part. But there is no hint of tentativeness in the tones of many ministers, officials and senior government advisers.

Despite assurances from official quarters, my unease and uncertainty remain. Are we experiencing the reprofessionalizing of teachers through the TTA's demanding new professional standards; the increased discretion given schools over the newly designated non-core subjects of the National Curriculum; the valuably detailed approaches of the National Literacy and Numeracy Projects; the comprehensive 'national' schemes of work in science and IT issued by QCA; and through the long-awaited setting up of a General Teaching Council?

Or are we experiencing the deprofessionalizing of teachers through a state-controlled programme of continuing professional development; moves to establish a 'neo-elementary' ITEMS-based curriculum; denial of teacher autonomy in teaching number, reading and writing and in planning science and IT; and through the absence of any substantial executive power in the General Teaching Council?

Primary education is at a hinge of history. Will that hinge open or shut doors to progress and development, in English primary education?

Author Index

Abbott, R. 45
Alexander, R. 36, 44, 49, 50, 77, 82, 91, 94, 97, 105–8, 119, 124
Ashton, P. 16, 20, 23
Auld, R. 16, 23

Bantock, G. 17, 23
Bassey, M. 20, 23
Bealing, D. 20, 23
Bell, D. 2
Bennett, N. 17, 19, 20, 23, 38, 44, 108
Bernbaum, G. 13, 23
Birchenough, C. 55, 56, 66
Blunkett, D. 96, 98
Blyth, W. 16, 17, 23, 36, 44, 57, 58, 66
Board of Education 56–7, 58, 66, 69, 72
Bolam, R. 45
Boyson, R. 16, 23
Bramwell, R. 55, 57, 66
Broadfoot, P. 33, 44
Browne, S. 18, 24
Burstall, C. 13, 24

Callaghan, J. 15, 24
Campbell, R. 41, 42, 44, 94, 98
Carroll, L. 132, 140
Central Advisory Council for Education (Plowden Report) 7–10, 24, 35, 44, 59, 61, 62, 66
Collings, H. 13, 24
Consultative Committee of the Board of Education 7–8, 12
Coulson, A. 43, 44
Cox, G. 16, 19
Croydon 39, 44

Daugherty, R. 129, 131
Dearing, R. 98
Department for Education and Employment 93, 94, 98, 133, 134, 135, 136–7, 138, 139, 140

Department of Education and Science 12, 13, 16, 17, 18, 20, 21, 24, 27, 28, 34, 36, 37, 38, 39, 40, 41, 44, 45, 62, 63, 66, 68, 69, 94, 98
Dickens, C. 139, 140
Dyson, T. 19

Exon, G. 45

Farrell 61, 97, 140
Fisher, S. 37, 45
Fogelman, K. 94, 98
Foxman, D. 136, 140

Galton, M. 19, 24, 94, 95, 96, 98
Gardener, D. 19, 24
Golby, M. 44, 45
Goldstein, H. 133, 140

Harlen, W. 17, 21, 24
Harwood, D. 37, 45
Hencke, D. 13, 24
Hewison, J. 42, 45
Hicks, D. 37, 45
Holley, B. 45
Holly, P. 45
Holmes, E. 56, 58, 66
Hopkins, D. 44, 45

ILEA 37, 45

Jamieson, I. 37, 45
Jinks, D. 37, 45

Keys, W. 136, 140

Lynch, J. 22, 24

MacDonald, B. 14, 21, 22, 24
Macleod, F. 42, 45

Subject Index